JAGUAR XJ-S

The Complete Story

GRAHAM ROBSON

Other Titles in the Crowood AutoClassics Series

JAGUAR XJ-S

The Complete Story

GRAHAM ROBSON

THE CROWOOD PRESS

First published in 1997 by
The Crowood Press Ltd
Ramsbury, Marlborough
Wiltshire SN8 2HR

www.crowood.com

Paperback edition 2007

© Graham Robson 1997

British Library Cataloguing-in-Publication Data
A catalogue record for this book is available from the British Library.

ISBN 978 1 86126 933 1

Typeface used: New Century Schoolbook.

Typeset and designed by D&N Publishing
Lambourn Woodlands, Hungerford, Berkshire.

Printed and bound by CPI Bath.

Contents

Acknowledgements

Although I did not start to write this book until 1996, the last year of the XJ-S's career, I have been a Jaguar-watcher for many years. Having started my career (pre-XJ-S!) at Browns Lane, and driven many Jaguars since then, I have also made friends with many Jaguar personalities who all helped, one way or another, to fill my memory banks with XJ-S facts, figures and impressions.

I couldn't possibly have written the book without a great deal of help from these kind people, some of whom are unhappily no longer with us. Special thanks, therefore, to: David Boole, Joe Greenwell, Colin Cook, Martin Broomer and Anne Harris of Jaguar Cars at Browns Lane; Graham Whitehead, Mike Cook, John Dugdale and Karen Miller of Jaguar Cars Inc. in the USA; Bill Donnelly at JaguarSport, Oxfordshire; Jaguar characters such as 'Lofty' England, Walter Hassan, Harry Mundy and Bob Knight; Geoffrey Robinson, MP – one-time Jaguar Chairman – for taking time out of a busy parliamentary schedule to see me; Michael Ware and his staff at the National Motor Museum, Beaulieu, for allowing me to dig deeply into the BP Library's records without supervision.

I am only sorry that Sir John Egan could not spare the time to tell me about his time at Jaguar in the 1980s.

Some time after the XJS dropped out of production, a rigorous recount of production figures was made, and is now reproduced on page 190. I am very grateful to Anders Clausager, Chief Archivist of the Jaguar Daimler Heritage Trust, for this material.

For every Jaguar enthusiast, all round the world, I hope this book gives a well-rounded summary of the life and times of a great car. If all of you get as much pleasure from driving XJ-Ss as I do, there will be many smiling faces at Jaguar gatherings for years to come.

Graham Robson, 1997

Introduction

This is the life story of Jaguar's most controversial car. On the one hand the XJ-S had a magnificent chassis, superb road manners and astonishing refinement. On the other, some people did not like the styling, and many of the earlier cars suffered quality defects. No one could ignore the XJ-S, and everyone seems to have definite opinions about it.

Straight away, this should tell you that my 'Complete Story' does not paint the picture of a car without blemish. However, the sales figures tell their own story, and Jaguar is proud of that. In a life of nearly twenty-one years, the XJ-S rose above every criticism, proved its point again and again, and is now remembered as a remarkable sporting Jaguar.

One factor above all others explains why there is something of a mid-Atlantic angle to this survey – almost exactly one in two XJ-S cars were originally delivered to the United States. That statistic, and the commercial realities behind it, explains why the XJ-S looked, behaved, and was specified in the way it was – and why I sought American as well as British insight when writing the story.

This book is not only about the cars themselves, but about the people involved in them.

Not only was the XJ-S the last car that Sir William Lyons influenced before his retirement, but it was committed to production by 'Lofty' England and Geoffrey Robinson, designed and developed by notable engineers led by characters such as Bob Knight and Harry Mundy, and nurtured throughout the 1980s by that extrovert manager, John Egan.

In a company like Jaguar, no single model can evolve without reference to the rest of the range and to the company's commercial fortunes. Because the XJ-S's career spanned several changes of company ownership (including a short and heady period of independence), several chief executives, profits and losses in profusion, the evolution of two widely different engine families and a final period of stability under Ford, this is a long, complex and fascinating story.

Looking back, it is remarkable that the XJ-S survived so many traumatic periods in Jaguar's history. It was a thirsty and expensive car launched at a time when such cars were deeply unpopular, and it came close to extinction in 1980 when Jaguar was in deep crisis, yet it flowered, and prospered mightily, in the expansive 1980s. Its final evolution only came about because Ford believed in it, and eventually proved their point.

Evolution

Jaguar XJ-S Evolution

Date	Event
Date	*Event*
1963/1964	Project work began on the 'XJ4' family of Jaguar saloons, which would eventually become the XJ6/XJ12 models.
1964	Four-cam V12 engine first ran on the test bed. The definitive single-cam production engine gradually evolved from this.
1968	Introduction of the new-generation XJ6 four-door saloon, on a 108.8in (2,764mm) wheelbase/platform. First thoughts, at Jaguar, on an E-Type replacement, later to be coded XJ27, later to become the XJ-S.
1971	Launch of the first-ever V12-engined Jaguar – the Series III E-Type. Serious development work on XJ27 (to become the XJ-S) began, using a 102in (2,591mm) wheelbase version of the XJ12's platform.
1972	Launch of the XJ12 saloon, still on the 108.8in (2,764mm) wheelbase.
September 1975	Introduction of the original XJ-S coupé, with 285bhp/5.3-litre V12 engine, and a choice of manual or automatic transmission.
March 1979	Manual gearbox option officially withdrawn.
July 1981	Introduction of XJ-S HE (High Efficiency) model, with 299bhp.
October 1983	Introduction of XJ-S 3.6-litre models, with new-type AJ6 six-cylinder engine and manual transmission, and a choice of coupé and cabriolet body styles.
July 1985	Introduction of the cabriolet body style with the V12 engine.
September 1987	XJ-S 3.6 Cabriolet discontinued.
February 1988	XJ-S V12 Cabriolet discontinued.

Date	Event
March 1988	Introduction of the XJ-S V12 Convertible. No six-cylinder engined convertible at this stage.
April 1991	Introduction of 'facelifted' XJ-S series, with modified cabin and rear-end styles. Different shape side glass on coupés, different tail lamps and rear panels on all types. V12 engine continued at 5.3 litres, now re-rated at 290bhp. Six-cylinder engine enlarged to 4.0litres/223bhp.
May 1992	Introduction of new six-cylinder derivative, the 4.0-litre/223bhp car, complete with automatic transmission option, and a convertible body option.
May 1993	Final facelift, plus 6.0-litre/308bhp V12 engine, plus four-speed automatic transmission.
June 1994	Major revisions for 4.0-litre/six-cylinder models, now with AJ16-type engine, and 241bhp.
End 1995	Final V12 engined XJS models produced.
April 1996	Final XJS of all produced. Replaced by new XK8 range.

XJR-S models, as produced by JaguarSport

August 1988	First XJR-S introduced, mechanically as the XJ-S V12 model, but with revised suspension and a 'dress-up' kit. Only available as a coupé.
September 1989	Original XJR-S replaced by XJR-S 6.0-litre, with 318bhp engine. At first only available in the UK.
May 1990	XJR-S 6.0-litre also made available in Europe.
Spring 1991	XJR-S 6.0-litre made available with facelifted bodystyle.
Autumn 1991	Introduction of revised XJR-S 6.0-litre, with 333bhp.
Spring 1992	XJR-S 6.0-litre introduced to USA.
May 1993	XJR-S models discontinued.

1 Coupé Jaguars – the XJ-S's Heritage

This is where the pedants will have a field day. According to some people, the Jaguar story began in 1945, while according to others it really started when the 'Jaguar' badge first appeared on the nose of an SS-Jaguar motor car. Even then, the arguments are not over, for those cars' ancestors, badged as SS models, had already been on sale for four years before that.

My own view is that the soul of all modern Jaguars stems from the original SS cars of 1931, so that is where this story really begins. From October 1931, when the prototype SSI was first seen at London's Olympia Motor Show, to the early 1970s, when the XJ-S was conceived, a series of companies were all run by the same man – William Lyons, who became Sir William when he was knighted in 1956.

The very first SS cars – like the Swallow-bodied cars that had preceded them – were a triumph of styling over engineering. As their performance improved, all that would change considerably during the marque's first decade, but in the beginning there is no doubt that an early SS looked a lot faster than it actually was. William Lyons, the thrusting young man who had started by shaping a series of smart motorcycle sidecars in Blackpool in the early 1920s, then progressed to styling smart new body shells for mundane cars like the Austin Seven, the Morris Cowley and the Standard Sixteen, knew all about this problem, but nonetheless shrugged it aside.

Even though the Swallow business had expanded considerably, and had been moved to Coventry at this stage in his career, neither he nor his limited team of colleagues at Swallow were yet capable of changing and improving the chassis on which they built bodies. That would follow, but for the moment Lyons concentrated on making a series of styles that were lower, sleeker and more rounded than their rivals. Initially these were two-door cars – open or closed – some undoubtedly being the very smartest coupés the British market had yet seen.

SSI – THE FIRST OF THE LINE

Naturally there was no technical connection between the original SSI of 1931 and the XJ-S of 1975, but it is extremely important to realize that Sir William Lyons was closely connected with them both. The fact is that until he officially retired from Jaguar in 1972, Sir William was the stylist, the artist, the arbiter of shape, packaging, equipment, fixtures and fittings, behind almost every SS, SS-Jaguar or Jaguar production. Experienced and expert designers have often told me that it is easy to spot the 'cues' with which Sir William came to shape his creations, and that it was simple enough to spot how one car was developed from the previous generation. Although the XJ-S was not finalized until he had stepped down from the chair at Jaguar, Sir William had

Jaguar's reputation was built on the success of the SS motor car. This was the original SS advertisement of October 1931, emphasizing that appearance would always mean much to William Lyons, and that coupés were his first love.

certainly been involved in the conception, the packaging and the general shaping of the car that came after his retirement.

The origins of the SSI are now very well known. By 1931 William Lyons and his partner William Walmsley had already turned the Swallow Coachbuilding Company into a prosperous business, and it was Lyons's ambition that sent it forward to greater expansion. In a unique co-operative deal with John Black and the Standard Motor Co. Ltd, Swallow arranged for Standard to supply complete six-cylinder rolling

chassis, on to which an entirely new type of body shell would be mounted. Even allowing for a gap of more than forty years, and for the different styling standards that applied, there were aspects of the first SSI style that could also be found in the XJ-S – if you know where to look for them.

However, it is also important to know that the first SSI prototype was completed while Lyons was away from work (he had been hospitalized after an appendix operation), so the car that appeared was by no means the one he had originally intended for launch.

For that reason, several observers look to the 1932/1933 SSI as the first *true* 'Lyons-SS', a car much improved in packaging and general detail. Then, as in the 1950s and 1960s, Lyons's eye for a line was not infallible, but he was persistent, and got there in the end. In his case, second or third thoughts were often better than the original – the difference being that by the 1960s he never allowed his original ideas to be seen in public, though a number of archive pictures have survived!

Let us therefore look at the 1932/1933 SSI to see what it tells us. First and foremost was the fact that this was a striking and very low car, totally dominated by its long bonnet. In this case, a long nose was actually necessary because of the bulk of the Standard six-cylinder engine that it covered, but that was immaterial: all the evidence is that Lyons preferred long noses to the more stubby variety. (Cars like the SSII and the 1½-litre SS Jaguars that followed never looked as balanced as their larger-engined relations.)

Having seen earlier artwork for the SSII, we know that Lyons would also have liked to make the roof line even lower than it actually was, but the practical need for some headroom meant that the roof was raised while he was in hospital being deprived of his appendix. (Having seen the completed car, when it was too late to make pre-Olympia

Study this shot of a 1933-vintage SSI coupé, and you will see many of the features which would re-appear in the XJ-S of the mid-1970s, including the long bonnet, the small 2+2-seater cabin and the dramatic visual detailing.

Show changes, Lyons is reputed to have exclaimed: 'It looks like a conning tower!' Even so, the motoring correspondent of the *Daily Express*, Harold Pemberton, later wrote that:

> The new motor-car is certainly the lowest-built British car I have ever seen...

which confirms how different it was from the usual British standard of the day.

The side view showed long, flamboyant, sweeping lines that were much more eloquent that most of the competition's, and certainly made the SSI look like a performance car, even when parked at the kerbside. In particular, the crown-line of the front wings was elegant and carefully detailed, as was all the detailing of the nose, the badging and the lamps.

Even in revised, 1932/1933 form, the SSI's four-seater cabin was distinctly cramped, with enough space for front seat passengers, but precious little for those who had to sit in the rear. Front-seat passengers got good all-round visibility, but rear-seat passengers were in semi-privacy. Rear-seat leg space? According to the diagram published in The *Autocar's* road test, if the front seats were pushed back there was only 5.5in (140mm) between the squab and the front of the rear seat cushion.

Analysing the SSI in considerable detail is worthwhile because of its similarities with later Jaguar coupés, especially the XJ-S. Like the SSII, the XJ-S was very low, with a long and impressive bonnet. Although in 1975 it might not have been lower than its competitors, it was still miraculously well-packaged, especially with the mass of that complicated V12 engine to be hidden.

Then there were the lines along the flanks. You might not be a great fan of the 'sail panels' that linked the roof of the XJ-S to the tail (but then, was that any more contrived than the false hood-folding irons

Sir William Lyons (1901–85)

Blackpool-born William Lyons founded the Swallow sidecar building business with William Walmsley, then followed up with SS Cars, before becoming sole proprietor in 1935. He invented the Jaguar marque name in 1935, saw his company become world-famous after World War Two, and was 'Mr Jaguar' until the day he retired in 1972.

During his working life William Lyons, who had a faultless eye for the right line despite his lack of formal training, shaped every Jaguar production car except the E-Type (which was a direct evolution of the D-Type, and therefore Malcolm Sayer's responsibility).

This ensured that there was always an evolutionary connection between one Jaguar and the next, and it meant that 'the Jaguar look' was always instantly recognizable all over the world. Today's designers can still see styling 'cues' that link the SS cars of the 1930s with the Mark VII of the 1950s, and with the XJ6 of the 1960s. Sir William even insisted that the XK engine should look right as well as being very powerful! Although the XJ-S style had not been finalized before he retired in 1972, many of his likes and dislikes were clearly evident in the new car's lines.

Sir William (he was knighted in 1956) was always respected by his workforce, though never loved, as he was reputedly a hard taskmaster. He liked to keep a formal atmosphere in his business, calling even his closest colleagues by their surnames and keeping them personally at arm's length. Some of this reserve was almost certainly caused by the death of his only son (and heir) and his need to make sure that he showed no personal or business favours to anyone.

Not only was Sir William an accomplished and successful stylist, he was also an astute businessman, and a talented chooser of staff. It was no accident that Jaguar Cars grew and prospered while rival companies (Daimler and Armstrong-Siddeley being perfect examples) struggled to survive.

To underpin Jaguar's future after he had gone, Sir William agreed to merge with BMC in 1966, this then leading to his company becoming a part of British Leyland in 1968. Until the day he retired, however, Sir William protected the technical and styling independence of his cars – the merger with Daimler, for instance, leading to Jaguar ideas being incorporated into Daimler cars, but not the other way around.

After retiring, he continued to visit the factory that he had built up, and he was always involved with the development and finalization of the XJ-S. It is known, too, that he took a close interest in the development of the new-generation AJ6 engine. Though he was known to be disappointed by the fallow years that followed British Leyland's traumas, before he died, at eighty-four, he was once again content to see Jaguar privatized and prospering.

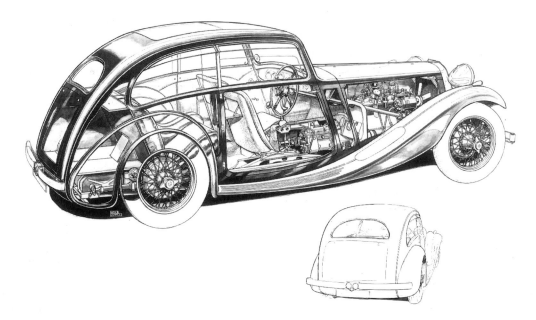

The SS Airline of the mid-1930s was shaped by William Lyons, and although it was a four-seater the rear-seat passengers were not provided with much space. Not much changed, then in the next forty years!

found on the SSI?), but you had to agree that this was an extremely sleek style that made the most of its proportions.

Finally, of course, there was the size of the cabin. The XJ-S, let me remind you, was 16ft (4,877mm) long, yet was still a car in which the cabin was a close-coupled four-seater. Cars had got a lot wider since 1932, of course, but they were also lower (the roof of the XJ-S was actually 5in (127mm) lower than that of the SSI ...). A look at *Autocar's* 1976 road test confirmed that the XJ-S's rear seat might have been 6in (152mm) wider than that of the SSI, but that there was 4.5in (114mm) less headroom, and 6in (152mm) less front-to-back space. Memory tells me, in fact, that when the front seats were pushed all the way back they actually touched the rear seat cushions.

Sir William Lyons, Jaguar's founder, governing director and chief stylist, ruled the company personally until the day he retired in 1972. Along with Malcolm Sayer, his final major styling project was the XJ-S.

14

Are there any lessons to be learned? There are, I think – mainly that Sir William's idea of how he wanted to make a coupé look did not change much over the years, that he was always happy to allow the styling to get in the way of what modern engineers would call 'packaging', and that he really did not have much interest in the plight of back seat passengers!

COUPÉ DEVELOPMENTS UNTIL THE 1960s

After the mid-1930s, when SS turned into SS-Jaguar, the cars were growing up fast, and it was no longer possible to buy close-coupled four-seaters. Late 1930s SS-Jaguars were either fully fledged four-door saloons or drop-head coupés, or (very rare, these) two-seater open sports cars, and the same range was built in the 1940s and 1950s.

The XK140 fixed-head coupé and the XK150 that followed in the 1950s both had so-called rear seats, but for a rear seat passenger it helped not to have legs, or to be willing to ride alone, sideways, and in acute discomfort. The E-Type 2+2 of 1966 was even less practical. The rear seat, such as it was, had virtually no rear leg space when the front seats were pushed all the way back, while the headroom was severely restricted: not only that, but altering the wheelbase and the sweep of the roof line to accommodate '+2' seating marred the E-Type's otherwise superlative good looks.

In Europe, on the other hand, several manufacturers had produced good-looking and practical 2+2 coupés – Alfa Romeo and Lancia among them – and we now know

By the 1950s, Jaguar was making many more saloons than coupés, but the XK sports car had grown up to include this 2+2 coupé. The rear seat, though, was only really usable by children.

Earlier famous Jaguar coupés

Surprisingly, until the XJ-S came along, Jaguar had not made many 2+2 coupés. The bodywork slipping smoothly along behind the leaping cat has usually covered four-door saloons, or two-seaters with an open or metal top.

The first 2+2 model – though it was not badged as a Jaguar – was the original SSI of 1931, a car with such a long bonnet and small cabin that it was nearly a caricature. That was a car with a side-valve six-cylinder engine, and with only 45bhp and a 70mph (113km/h) top speed, it looked a lot faster than it actually was.

Several versions were built before the 'Jaguar' name arrived, but then there was a long gap. In fact the very first Jaguar-badged 2+2 coupé was the 2+2 E-Type of 1966, but if you were the fully grown passenger allocated to sit in the rear seats it helped to have universally jointed legs. I once travelled from Coventry to London in the back of such an E-Type, and wished I had not. I am glad there was only one rear seat passenger, because the legroom ahead of my seat was just 3in (75mm). The compensation, of course, was that this E-Type had a 265bhp/4.2-litre engine, and a 140mph (225km/h) top speed.

Which brings us to the only true (that is, practically packaged) Jaguar 2+2 to be on sale before the XJ-S. Amazingly, this did not go on sale until the spring of 1975, only months before the XJ-S arrived, and was really a full four-seater with a two-door cabin. It was, of course, the XJ-C, which was available with 170bhp (DIN)/4.2-litre or 285bhp (DIN)/5.3-litre power.

But here is a paradox. The V12-engined version, the XJ 5.3C, was a near-150mph (240km/h) car with considerably more space in the cabin that the XJ-S, and in 1975 (when both cars were newly on the market) it was £1,328 cheaper. Yet the XJ5.3C was a marketing failure (only 1,873 were sold in two years), whereas the XJ-S was a lasting success …

This was all the rear-seat accommodation that was on offer in the E-Type of the late 1960s and early 1970s. For the XJ-S, therefore, Jaguar was determined to do much better than this.

Immediately before the XJ-S went on sale, Jaguar's fastest sporting coupé was the E-Type Series III, which had the new 5.3-litre V12 engine. As with the XK150, however, the '+2' accommodation was strictly limited.

that Sir William Lyons, aided and abetted by his aerodynamicist Malcolm Sayer, kept on returning to the concept, to see if Jaguar could match these efforts.

In modern 'product-planning-speak', the market place for expensive, exclusive, restricted-seating coupés was not large, but at the time all the signs were that it was expanding, particularly in North America and Western Europe.

In affluent countries, more and more drivers found themselves with enough money to indulge themselves. They tended to be of

a recognizable type – usually married, with grown-up children, and now ready to enjoy themselves. Perhaps for the first time, they were earning enough to have money left over for fun. Once they had needed cars with four or five seats, four doors and cavernous boots, but this was all past. Now they had different needs – performance before economy, style before accommodation, and individuality above all.

Gradually but insidiously, Sir William Lyons became convinced that a slightly larger and reshaped E-Type 2+2 was not what he needed. For the mid-1970s, he concluded, Jaguar needed to return to its SS styling roots. Crucially, he decided to do this by making a big car smaller, rather than by enlarging a two-seater coupé.

If there was one single car that convinced him that a 1970s Jaguar coupé should be a genuine 2+2 rather than a stretched (and cramped) two-seater, it was the Mercedes-Benz 350SLC. Revealed in October 1971 – when work on the car which became the XJ-S was still not finalized – the 350SLC was *exactly* the sort of car Sir William

thought Jaguar needed. The 350SLC (which soon spawned larger-engined derivatives) was a thoroughly versatile 2+2 seater coupé with rather square and craggy styling, yet could exceed 130mph (210km/h) in original form, in near-silence and in great dignity.

Although Jaguar did not mention it at the time, this was precisely what a new 1970s Jaguar coupé was also meant to do, and from that moment development went ahead rapidly. Even so, to get the design settled would take years – as the following chapters make clear.

The XJ12C went on sale in the spring of 1975, being a shorter-wheelbase two-door version of the original XJ12 four-door saloon. Larger than the XJ-S, but with the same basic drive line and running gear, the XJ12C sold surprisingly slowly, and was dropped in 1977.

British Leyland attempted to turn the XJ12C into a successful race car in 1976 and 1977, but the project was always defeated by the car's great weight and its rather cumbersome handling. The XJ-S race cars of the mid-1980s would be much more successful than this.

'Coupé' – what's in a name?

A coupé is not a saloon, and it is not a sports car. It can be a fixed-head or a drop-head car, but it is not a tourer, and it is certainly not a cabriolet either. It is usually smaller, more sporting and with a smaller cabin than a full-size saloon. More importantly – you will recognize one when you see one.

Translation from the French is simple enough, so I am happy to say it means 'cut' or 'short'. By definition, therefore, a coupé is really a shortened or cut-down version of a saloon car, or perhaps a shortened version of a full-size cabriolet.

By my standards, too, coupés can only have two passenger doors, and certainly no more than four seats. I know that this clashes with some American usage, where a so-called 'hard-top' coupé can have four passenger doors, and space for six passengers. But then, the Americans have always been used to thinking big.

I am only labouring this point to make it clear that Jaguar actually made very few real coupés over the years …

2 XJ6 and XJ12 Saloons – the XJ-S's Building Blocks

Critics of the XJ-S, and its dependence on XJ6 and XJ12 saloon car engineering, should remember one basic fact – that without basing the XJ-S's design on that of those cars, it could never have gone on sale. Jaguar, quite simply, could never have afforded to finance a radically new car at the time. Money – or the lack of it – was a major factor that shaped the XJ-S, and this needs to be addressed at once. Although many books have been written about Jaguar cars, little space has ever been devoted to the company's finances. Yet here was a company that achieved so much, always with such limited resources.

Perhaps it wasn't Jaguar's ability to produce such stunning-looking cars, all of them with high performance and unmatchable character, that was the miracle of the post-war years. The miracle was actually being able to finance them and to stay afloat – and independent – for so long.

The fact is that although Jaguar was consistently profitable in the 1950s and 1960s, its maximum yearly profit was £1.66 million, recorded in 1966. Throughout this time the investment needed to tool up for a new car – investment in body press tools, machine tools, fixtures and facilities – rose rapidly. Even in the late 1950s, Sir William Lyons told his workforce that he would have to find £1 million so that Pressed Steel could start producing Mk X saloon shells. No figure for XJ6 costs was ever published, but it was unlikely to be less than £10 million.

All of this should explain why, when the time came, the XJ-S had to evolve around a modified version of the XJ6/XJ12 saloon's platform and running gear, but using a totally different 2+2 coupé body style. It was the only practical and financially prudent way that a 'successor' to the E-Type could be developed.

ENGINE AND CHASSIS ORIGINS

Although the XJ-S Coupé would eventually go on sale in the autumn of 1975, its mechanical origins – chassis/platform, engine and running gear – had actually been settled many years earlier. In many ways, the running gear, if not the styling, of the XJ-S had its origins in the 1960s.

To be specific, the pressed-steel platform (or underframe) dated back to 1964, the rear suspension design was first seen in 1961, the very first V12 engine ran in 1964, the four-speed all-synchromesh gearbox was launched in the same year, and the Borg Warner Model 12 Automatic gearbox had been fitted to many cars since the 1960s.

As everyone surely knows, the basis of the XJ-S design, the building block around which the entire car took place, was a shortened version of the XJ6's platform, and it is with this car that I start my search for the XJ-S's origins.

The XJ6, in fact, was launched in 1968, and was the first all-new Jaguar body/chassis to appear for seven years (the previous all-new shell being the Mk X of 1961). Its arrival was timely, for Jaguar's range of saloon cars had become over-complicated during the 1960s, and it was time for rationalization. Cleverly and cannily, Sir William got together with his technical chief, Bill Heynes, to develop a new car that would achieve that, and eventually take over from *all* the older models – whether Mk 2 or Mark X based.

Although the original XJ6 used a familiar power train – the six-cylinder twin-cam XK engine, a choice of Jaguar all-synchromesh manual or Borg Warner automatic transmissions, and a robust sub-frame mounted final drive – the platform/monocoque and the suspensions were new.

XJ6 Platform – Squat and Refined

In its original form, the XJ6's pressed platform had a wheelbase of 108.8in (2,763mm), along with front and rear wheel tracks of 58in (1,473mm). Not only did this give the new executive saloon a very stable base, one that could ride and handle well if Jaguar's engineers worked their usual miracle on damper and suspension mounting settings, but it also gave space for a full five-seater cabin to be arranged above it.

The cabin, in fact, was generously wide, if not overly long (which might explain why Jaguar decided to produce a longer-wheelbase version of the same machine a few years down the line). In the front seat area, in fact, the cabin was 54in (1,372mm) wide at shoulder height: this, incidentally, was 6in (152mm) more than the same measurement in the last of the E-Types, which shows at least one way in which Jaguar could improve its sporting-car line-up in the 1970s.

It was in the detailing of the suspension, however, that the XJ6 was so outstanding – detail that would be so advantageous when the XJ-S came to evolve. Although these units looked familiar enough – conventional, even, by 1960s Jaguar standards – in terms of ride and refinement, they were a generation ahead.

At the front, the coil spring/wishbone front suspension looked similar to earlier Jaguar types; it had anti-dive geometry and long wishbone links to allow a great deal of wheel movement, which allowed a soft ride at town speeds. The dampers, too, were positioned outboard of the coil springs, which allowed them to be much longer, and therefore to give more precise control. Not only that, but the suspension was mounted on a massive pressed steel box-section cross member, this itself being fixed to the monocoque through rubber mounting members.

At the rear, the independent suspension was mounted inside a pressed-steel bridge-type sub-frame, with twin spring/damper units at each side, all kept in check by forward-facing radius arms.

All this, linked to the use of power-assisted rack-and-pinion steering, 15in wheels with 6in rims and 70 per cent low-profile radial ply tyres, and with a huge amount of time devoted to tailoring the rates of the various rubber mounting bushes, gave the XJ6 a quite unrivalled combination of ride, handling and refinement. At the time, it was agreed, this set new world standards, which not even Rolls-Royce, Mercedes-Benz or Cadillac could match.

When the time came to develop the XJ-S, this remarkable platform would form an ideal base. Not only would it allow Jaguar to offer a much more spacious cabin than the 2+2 E-Type, but it would also promise a much better blend of ride, handling, roadholding and refinement. This was a mouthwatering prospect.

Browns Lane

Although all SS cars, all SS-Jaguars, and the early post-war Jaguars were produced at the Foleshill factory, this was bursting at the seams by 1950, and William Lyons began to look around for more factory space in Coventry. At this time the city was going through something of an industrial upheaval, not only because wholesale rebuilding to repair World War Two bomb damage was under way, but also because several of the original aero-engine shadow factories were becoming redundant.

The government's shadow factory scheme was launched in 1936, as a way of boosting the re-armament programme and particularly to get the motor industry involved in setting up, running and managing new aero-engine factories. No sooner was the first wave of factories up and running, than the government initiated phase two, the result being that Daimler built 'Shadow No. 2' in Browns Lane, Allesley, a few miles to the west of Coventry. This building began by manufacturing Bristol Hercules radial engines during the war, but by the early 1950s it was closed down, Daimler having no further use for it.

After a great deal of negotiation with government officials, William Lyons was able to buy (not lease, which was more normal at this period in government history) the factory. He began moving his assembly facilities into place during 1952 and completed the move by the end of that year. Once the move was completed, the Foleshill factory was sold off and all links with the SS and SS-Jaguar days on that site were dissolved.

Browns Lane has been the home of Jaguar ever since then, though it has been modified, expanded, rejigged and persistently modernized continuously. The purchase of the Daimler business, and its factories in Radford, Coventry, and the opening up of the technical centre at Whitley, Coventry, have not changed that. Every XJ-S, of whatever type, was completed at Browns Lane.

Even as recently as 1991, the city council opened a new road linking the Allesley by-pass to Brownshill Green, in which a major feature was a new roundabout and direct access to the old 'back gate', now the official 'new' main entrance to Browns Lane.

Ford, who controlled Jaguar after 1989, immediately laid plans to invest in Browns Lane to produce ever more cars in the late 1990s and 2000s. The first benefit came with approval to launch the much-revised XJ-S of 1991, then came the installation of new final assembly lines, while the launch of the XJ-S's replacement, the XK8, was a further, major phase.

V12 Engine: Complex Origins

When the new XJ6 was launched, it was only available with the long-established six-cylinder XK engine, but development was already well-advanced on a new family of closely related V8 and V12 engines. In due course the V8 version would be abandoned (at the time, Jaguar was not happy with the lack of refinement of what was a 60-degree design), but the V12 was eventually launched in 1971.

By this time, V12 engines – either on paper or in the metal – had been around at Jaguar for well over ten years. Even when I worked as a young designer at Jaguar in the late 1950s, the first XK-derived 60-degree V12 engine had already been schemed out, though no parts had been cast, forged, or machined.

At first this engine was meant to be a formidable racing engine, for use in future Jaguar long-distance racing sports cars. In its original 'paper' guise it was a 5-litre unit, the 60-degree V angle being chosen because it would give the best possible combination of balance and packaging.

Progress was slow. First thoughts (sketches, really) on a new mid-engined XJ13 racing sports car came in 1960, but this was never a priority project and the original V12 engine did not run on the test-

The very early Jaguar V12s were twin-cam units in the mid-1960s, racing units built to power the still-born mid-engined XJ13 sports car. The series-production V12 was a lineal development of that unit, this being an early six-SU, still with twin overhead camshafts per bank.

bed at Browns Lane until August 1964. At this time the twin-cam cylinder heads used 'downdraught' inlet ports (which meant that the manifolds were atop the heads and between the lines of the camshafts), and Lucas fuel injection was being used. Peak power was a brawny 502bhp at 7,600rpm, and there is little doubt that this would have provided Jaguar with race-winning performance if the XJ13 project had ever been completed.

The mid-engined XJ13, however, was never seriously developed, and after being run at MIRA during 1967 (where it set an unofficial outer circuit lap record that was not broken until 1990s supercars like the Jaguar XJ220 and the McLaren F1 came along) it was retired.

In the next few years, though, Sir William Lyons adopted the V12 layout for future production cars. He instructed his top designers, Walter Hassan and Harry Mundy, to transform the V12 into a powerful, ultra-reliable and silky-smooth road-car unit. This was not going to be easy, as the original V12 was a peaky, expensive-to-build, monster – too heavy, too complex and not nearly civilized enough for use in road cars.

In the end it took four years to develop, the result being the world's first quantity-production V12 unit of post-war years – Ferrari and Lamborghini V12s did not count, as these were produced by hand, by craftsmen, using the minimum of tooling.

Along the way, the engine lost its down-draught twin-cam cylinder heads and its Lucas fuel injection, for the Hassan/Mundy team (which had not designed the original

engine!) concluded that it lacked top end power *and* mid-range torque. The result was the choice of single-cam heads with a line of in-line valves and a more conventional fuel supply featuring four constant-vacuum Zenith-Stromberg carburettors, a type which had already proved very suitable for cars being sent to the increasingly exhaust emissions-conscious North American market. At the same time, to improve low-speed torque, the engine was given a larger bore, and enlarged from 4,994cc to 5,343cc.

Harry Mundy (1914–88)

The design of the Jaguar V12 engine in conjunction with Walter Hassan was the high point of Harry Mundy's impressive career, not only as a design engineer, but as a journalist.

Born in Coventry, educated in the city, then apprenticed to Alvis, he joined ERA in 1936 and spent a short time with Morris Engines (also in Coventry) before joining the RAF as an engineer officer during World War Two. After the War, he joined the design team at BRM, working on the controversial V16 Grand Prix car, but in 1950 Walter Hassan persuaded him to join him at Coventry-Climax as his chief designer.

In five short years at Coventry-Climax, Harry not only laid out the FWA sportscar engine, the stillborn 2.5-litre FPE V8 F1 engine, and the famous family of FPF twin-cam racing engines, but was also involved in designing other industrial engines.

He joined *The Autocar* as technical editor in 1955, and became a somewhat tempestuous journalist for nine years, during which time he also schemed up the original Lotus-Ford twin-cam engine which came to be used in famous cars like the Lotus Elan, the Ford Cortina-Lotus, and the Ford Escort Twin-Cam. His irascible, irrepressible character soon became a legend in the motor industry.

Walter Hassan then persuaded him to return to Coventry, where he became Jaguar's executive director of power unit design, and headed a design team that developed the new V12 engine, converting it from a racing twin-cam to a quantity-production single-cam variety. Later, he also initiated design work on the new-generation AJ6 family of six-cylinder engines, which were used in the XJ-S from 1983, these being launched after he had retired.

He retired from Jaguar in 1980 and died in 1988, aged seventy-two.

Sir William Lyons (right) and 'Lofty' England were the two principal Jaguar personalities who authorised development and production of the XJ-S in the early 1970s. 'Lofty' was managing director, then chairman, after Sir William retired.

(Opposite) As re-designed by Walter Hassan and Harry Mundy, the production-type V12 engine was introduced in March 1971. Here, in single-cam head form, with four-Zenith-Stromberg carburation, it was somehow squeezed into the engine bay of the E-Type.

As fitted to the XJ12 saloon, the new V12 engine completely filled the engine bay. Even though fuel injection would be fitted to the engine for its XJ-S application, there would be very little more space around the unit. The XJ12's engine bay got so hot, incidentally, that the battery (top right of this picture) was fitted with a cooling fan! One of the electronic 'black boxes' is positioned in the middle of the vee, an ideal place for it to overheat ...

Even in 1968, when the XJ6 was launched (but when neither the Series III E-Type nor the XJ-S models had even been designed), Jaguar briefed a few journalists, telling them that a V12 engine was being developed – but that it would not be ready for some time. At that time, it was scheduled only for use in a V12-engined XJ6, but this policy soon changed and it first appeared in March 1971, in the Series III E-Type.

XJ12 Saloon – XJ6 + V12 Engine

Much delayed because of the time taken to develop the engine, and by British Leyland's already obvious disorganization, the first Jaguar XJ12 saloon was not introduced until July 1972. It was altogether typical of British Leyland, too, that the launch occurred at the same as the Jaguar workforce chose to go on strike !

John Barber was Lord Stokes's right-hand-man during the early 1970s, and it was his recommendation that Jaguar should be subsumed into the rest of the cars divisions. Barber did not survive the trauma of nationalization, leaving the company immediately after the Ryder report was published.

After nationalization, Derek Whittaker got the unenviable job of running the unwieldy Leyland Cars business. Under Whittaker, Jaguar almost lost its independence.

When the XJ12 broke cover, after a considerable period of embargo, the Browns Lane workforce had already been on strike for four weeks. This dispute (over pay and conditions) then dragged on for a further six weeks, which meant that the first XJ12s did not reach their customers until October 1972. I find it highly significant that Sir William Lyons had recently retired, for under his control Jaguar had never had such a dispute and he would surely not have allowed it to drag on for so long.

Because the XJ6's platform, body style and engine had all been laid out to accommodate the new V12 engine, the XJ12 was always a very harmonious whole. Because there were virtually no style changes – you had to look very hard, and very closely, even to find the V12 badging – the only real way to 'pick' an XJ12 from an XJ6 was by observing its uncanny silence and smoothness – and seeing the major increase in performance.

In its original form, the 5.3-litre V12 produced 272bhp (DIN) at 5,850rpm in the Series III E-Type, and 265bhp (DIN) at 5,850rpm in the XJ12, the difference between the two cars being entirely down to the different and more comprehensive silencing system in the XJ12 saloon. If you take one look at the complex throttle linkage needed to control the Zenith-Stromberg carburettors – two of which were mounted at each side of the massive assembly – you can surely see why Walter Hassan would always have preferred to fit fuel injection from the very beginning!

In the XJ12, but not the Series III E-Type, the V12 engine was only available with automatic transmission. Jaguar's manual box was not strong enough.

Walter Hassan (1905–96)

The man who started his working life with Bentley in 1920, and who had still not ended it in the early 1990s, had three spells with SS Cars (later Jaguar Cars), which were bracketed by an equally illustrious period with Coventry-Climax. Not only was he a famous engine designer in the postwar years, but he was equally well known as a racing mechanic and as a special car builder in his younger years.

Walter Thomas Frederick Hassan, born and educated in London, joined Bentley at Cricklewood as an apprentice, eventually joined the racing team as a mechanic and went on to prepare special cars for Woolf Barnato and others in the 1930s. After working briefly at ERA, then at Thomson & Taylor (at Brooklands), he joined SS Cars as chief development engineer in 1938.

Following a brief spell with the Bristol Aeroplane Company during the Second World War, he returned to SS in 1943. After dabbling with the design of lightweight parachute-drop fighting vehicles, he became a founder member of the XK engine design and development team and came to run Jaguar's busy experimental department when the Mark V and Mark VII models were being finalized.

In 1950 he became Coventry-Climax's chief engineer, later technical director, where he masterminded the design of racing engines such as the FPE V8, the FPF four-cylinder, and the FWMV V8 designs. After Jaguar took over Coventry-Climax in 1963, he found himself with responsibilities on two sites.

Before returning to Jaguar, full-time, in 1966 as Group Chief Engineer, Power Units, he was always close to the finalization of the 4.2-litre engines and new transmissions used in mid-1960s Jaguars, and the design of the V12 engine. After taking over from Bill Heynes as engineering director in 1969, he saw the fabulous V12 engine safely into production, then finally retired from Jaguar in 1972.

The XJ12 saloon, launched in mid-1972, was the car on which the XJ-S Coupé design was based. In XJ12 form, though, there was a longer wheelbase, four passenger doors and a less powerful version of the engine.

PERFORMANCE, LUXURY AND REFINEMENT

In some ways, the launch of the V12-engined Series III E-Type of 1971 was something of a disappointment, for a number of experts condemned it for being no better than a re-engined six-cylinder E-Type: more than one summed up with the same aphorism, 'new wine, old bottle'!

On the other hand, once the general public got its hands on the XJ12 saloon in 1972, this luxurious new model created quite a stir, not only for its remarkable technical specification, but for its price – a mere £3,726.

Although well-signalled in the motoring press, this model was quite outstanding in everything but its fuel economy. Not only was it arguably the best-riding and most refined motor car in the early-1970s motoring world, but it also had quite startling performance. Although it weighed 3,900lb (1,773kg), an XJ12 had a top speed of nearly 150mph (240km/h) and could sprint from 0–100mph

in 19.0sec. That was the good news – the bad news was that XJ12s usually returned no more than 12mpg (23.5l/100km), which was bad enough while petrol prices were still low, but which would seem appalling after the Energy Crisis, and the price rises, of 1973/1974.

Autocar magazine's road testers summed up the XJ12's character by commenting on the:

Phenomenal performance ... but deplorable fuel consumption. Superb quietness and refinement ... A truly outstanding motor car ... the XJ12 is, like so many Jaguars before it, a car of great superlatives. It is a marvellous achievement, deservedly the envy of the world.

This was typical of the world's reaction to the combination of the V12 engine in an advanced monocoque chassis, which was very encouraging for Jaguar and their engineering team. Unknown to the world, they had been working away on a new sporting coupé for some time – one that would combine all the virtues of the XJ12 but that would have a startling new style. Although it was still three years away, the XJ-S was on the way.

(Facing page, top) The XJ12C was previewed in 1973, when it still had a carburetted V12 engine, but finally went on sale in 1975, complete with a fuel-injected engine. This cutaway drawing of the carburettor-equipped prototype shows the layout of the running gear, which would also be used on the XJ-S Coupé, to be announced a few months later.

(Facing page, bottom) Although the V12 engine was little longer than the existing XK six-cylinder unit, it was much bulkier in every other dimension. As fitted to the E-Type Series III, it was fitted with four Zenith-Stromberg carburettors.

3 XJ-S and the V12 Engine – Original Development

Even in the mid-1960s, Sir William Lyons's styling ideas were inching towards the eventual nose shape of the XJ-S, this being an early study of the four-door saloon which became the XJ6 saloon.

Although active development of the XJ-S did not begin until the 1970s, talk of replacing the E-Type – which was the rather tenuously connected Jaguar ancestor to the XJ-S – had been rife for several years before that. No sooner had the E-Type 2+2 been launched in 1966 than Jaguar seem to have started thinking about its successors. A number of archive pictures, drawings and personal reminiscence confirm this.

The E-Type 2+2, of course, was certainly not a direct ancestor of the XJ-S, for it used an entirely different mechanical base, had a much smaller cabin and was more overtly sporting. On the other hand, it was the only existing Jaguar '2+2' that Jaguar management could inspect at the time, and around which discussions could begin. The complication, too, was that although the XJ6 saloon (on which the XJ-S would eventually be based) eventually appeared as a full-size five-seater saloon, the first styling studies were actually made on the basis of an enlarged E-Type!

This, in fact, was always Mission Impossible. Studies for a successor to the E-Type 2+2 were almost impossibly difficult to tackle at first. For the future, how on earth could any stylist reconcile the need for a larger cabin, a smaller front overhang, and yet keep the suggestion of the E-Type's sinuous lines? At that original stage in the late 1960s, there was no intention to produce a brand new shape, and certainly not to base a new car on the still-secret XJ6/XJ12 floorpan.

After the formation of BMH (British Motor Holdings) by the merger of Jaguar with BMC (a Corporation that not only made a multitude of family cars, but also made Austin-Healey and MG sports cars), the first tentative ideas of rationalizing the corporation's sports cars began to develop. All manner of oddities were investigated by BMH at this stage – at least on paper – including

Jaguar's Browns Lane factory was bursting at the seams in the mid-1970s when the XJ-S first went into production. This aerial view shows the way that Jaguar had added to the war-time buildings (the central block, with dark roofs) over the years, but that they were running out of space to expand. Coventry city centre is in the distance, at the top of the picture, and the administration block (including Sir William's office) is left foreground.

projects such as much-modified MGB GTs using bulky Daimler 4½-litre V8 engines!

XJ21 AND XJ27

Then came the genesis of a new project at Jaguar, which was coded XJ21. Although this was not the birth of a new car, it can generally be considered as the basis of an E-Type replacement. By 1968 the designers were looking at 'paper motor cars' with 2+2 and full four-seater cabins, with old-type six-cylinder XK or even new-generation V8/V12 engines. This was progress at last, but very haltingly, without urgency, and without proper direction.

After the formation of British Leyland in 1968, Jaguar's identity was submerged still further into an amorphous and somewhat disorganized structure, yet the design team worked steadily ahead, more work was done, and for the very first time the XJ21, as it was still called, began to take on shapes far removed from those of the E-Type. These, however, were still only 'on paper', or as small-scale wooden models, rather than in the full-size flesh, as Sir William Lyons had not yet got around to having mock-ups built by Fred Gardner's secret development workshop.

By this time the final E-Type, the Series III, was evolving around the longer-wheel-base version of the original E-Type floorpan, with the multi-tubular front end much changed to allow fitment of the new V12 engine. This car, coded XJ25, might have been scheduled for production in 1970/1971,

The V12 engine was first seen in the E-Type Series III of 1971, but Jaguar's replacement for this car would be much larger, much less sporting and very different in its styling.

XJ-S versus E-Type Series III		
Dimensions in in/mm		
	XJ-S	*E-Type SIII*
Length	191.7/4,869	184.5/4,686
Width	70.6/1,793	66/1,676
Height	50/1,270	51/1,295
Wheelbase	102/2,591	105/2,667
Widest track	58.6/1,488	54.5/1,384
'Across shoulders' cabin width	55.5/1,410	48.0/1,219
Front-seat-to-rear-seat dimension (max)	24.5/622	22.0/559
Unladen weight	3,900lb/1,769kg	3,300lb/1,497kg

but there was still the intention of producing XJ21 within a year of that!

As the Series III E-Type neared production and all the problems inside British Leyland began to intensify, any thought of producing an XJ21 car was quietly abandoned. From 1968, after all, Sir William Lyons was no longer in total and unchallenged control of his own company, and British Leyland's chief executive, Sir Donald Stokes, was not willing to commit multi-million pound investment towards a new car whose features could not be shared across the British Leyland range.

By 1970, however, it was already certain that a new sporting Jaguar model would not be developed from the E-Type's structure, as that was not only old-fashioned in engineering terms, but was considered rather too cramped. To quote one comment Lofty England made, many years after his retirement from the Jaguar chair:

The V12 was never supposed to go in the E-Type in the first place. Because the future project, the XJ-S, was some way off, it got into the E-Type. The E-Type was never designed for the V12 engine, or the other way round, of course. It was good luck that we managed to get it in.

But one of the biggest failings of the E-Type was the fact that you hadn't got enough room in the scuttle to get a decent air conditioning set-up in there, which is pretty vital, and this is the reason why we went to the XJ-S.

As to the final decision to drop the E-Type, you can blame this on me. I loved E-Types – beautiful – but they had these deficiencies. People don't realize how operating conditions have changed since 1961. Traffic is now so appalling, and you spend half your time sitting in a traffic jam. If you're sitting in traffic, you need some room to move and you need a proper, decent air conditioning system. The E-Type hadn't got it.

Thus it was that the general requirement for a car 'to replace the E-Type' – I put that phrase in inverted commas because there was no way that a much larger, heavier and bulkier car could ever replace the E-Type – began to take shape. It was generally agreed that, as XJ27, this would use only the V12 engine (the old XK six-cylinder unit was never seriously considered, not even in the depths of the Energy Crisis of 1973/1974). Even though the popularity of closed E-Type SIIIs was rapidly declining while the

This late-1960s mock-up shows how the E-Type might have been enlarged. This particular model – it never became a running car – has a larger cabin than the existing E-Type 2+2, a modified rear style and an entirely new nose which is remarkably similar to the Maserati Ghibli of the period.

XJ27 project took shape – the very last of these cars were built in October 1973, which meant that only open-top E-Types were built thereafter – open-top versions of XJ27 were apparently never seriously considered at the time. No matter what schemes were made, it seems that every early-1970s prototype was a closed car of the type we now know so well.

In view of this car's obvious competition – the W107 Mercedes-Benz 350SL/450SL range, which had been introduced in 1971 – that was amazing. In that case, open and closed, two-seater or four-seater versions were all available from the start, *and it was*

the closed, SLC, variety that died away in 1981. Who was right therefore – Jaguar or Mercedes-Benz?

The answer is that both firms were in fact correct. In the four-year gap between the launch of the Mercedes-Benz car and the Jaguar, the market place in the United States changed completely, and since the North American market was always critical to the XJ27's success, designers had to take account of what was brewing. Quite simply, there were serious moves to ban the sale of open-top cars in North America! Long-time president of British Leyland's North American subsidiary, Graham Whitehead, told me:

The opposition! The Mercedes-Benz 350SLC and 450SLC coupé models, launched in 1971, were exactly the sort of car that Jaguar was aiming to replicate with the XJ-S, offering 2+2 seating and high equipment levels. Like the XJ-S, the 450SLC was aimed squarely at the affluent North American market.

Settling the layout of the XJ-S was a problem, because we had really been asking for a sports car to replace the E-Type. It's difficult to remember the exact chronology, but there were certain federal laws being promulgated – there was a particular one in Ohio, I believe – about convertibles. It was not going to be possible to sell convertibles.

It was eventually decided that new safety standards could not be written in such a way that convertibles would be rendered illegal – but by that time Jaguar had already gone down the road to develop the XJ-S as a fixed-head coupé.

Mike Cook, equally long-serving USA-based Jaguar PR man, also recalls the legislative problem:

Jaguar were originally looking at developing coupés and convertibles, rather than roadsters and fixed-heads ...
[to an American, there is a world of difference between a 'convertible', and a 'roadster' – the 'roadster' traditionally having a less luxuriously trimmed, usually smaller cabin, with a less complex fold-away soft-top].
Jaguar has continually gone up-market throughout the whole history of the

company, so moving out of a two-seater sports car into a 2+2 GT car was just another step up-market.

At the time there was pressure in the federal government for legislation which would ban convertibles. This would not only affect the XJ27 project, it would also affect the TR7 and the MGB ...

Basically what happened is that it was proposed that in the Federal Safety regulations there would be one that would ban convertibles because of the rollover protection case. It was going to establish a rollover standard, which would mean that a convertible would have to have a roll cage in it.

This was going to be expensive to build and so hard to market that car companies began to design closed coupés. All of this happened in the early 1970s, so Jaguar was looking down the road at the impossibility of being able to market an open-top car – so the XJ-S became a coupé.

That federal proposal got dumped in the Federal Court in Cincinatti in 1973 – just at the wrong time for Jaguar and Triumph – the judgement being that it was not the business of the US government to tell people

Who can say if Jaguar was not influenced, at least, by the rather angular style of the Mercedes-Benz 350SLC and 450SLC models, which were direct rivals to the XJ-S? In the 1970s and in the 1990s, Jaguar always saw the German marque as their main competition.

what model of car they could buy. That struck it down, there was no appeal and no struggle, so once again the field was open – but that was 1973 and people had already been engineering new coupés for two years.

Triumph got the TR7 Convertible on sale by 1979, but for Jaguar the first open XJ-S would be the Cabriolet, which didn't come until the 1984 model year. No sun-roof even!

In the meantime, and well before the style of XJ27 was settled, Jaguar had decided to use the newfangled V12 engine – but there was much to be done before this could be ready.

V12 ENGINE – A DIFFICULT BIRTH

Although the very first Jaguar V12 engine existed on paper by the early-1950s, a V12 did not actually go on sale until 1971. Even by modern standards, when emission testing gets in the way of speedy progress, that was a very long time indeed.

Car enthusiasts who have never worked in the motor industry may not understand this. Why does it take so long to turn a 'good idea' into hardware? Sometimes, one admits, there is no good reason apart from changed priorities or a lack of capital, but in this case there were several. The very first V12 design never progressed beyond a number of drawings, the second racing design was not then done until the mid-1960s, and a redesign for series-production purposes did not follow until 1967–1968.

In the beginning the very first Jaguar V12 engine was schemed up as a racing unit in 1951, though not in great detail, and a more serious study followed in the mid-1950s. If you look back at 1950s racing trends it is easy to see why. When Jaguar won the Le Mans 24-hour race in 1951, its 3.4-litre XK engines

produced about 200bhp, this being ample to win the race and give the C-Type two-seaters a near-150mph (240km/h) top speed.

Ferrari, Jaguar's major competitor, then began developing larger and ever-more powerful V12s of their own. By 1953 the Type 375MM produced 340bhp and in 1954 the monstrous 4.9-litre cars had even more, with colossal torque. There was more to come, for in 1955 Jaguar's latest D-Types (still with 'only' 270bhp) had to face up to Mercedes-Benz 300SLRs that produced 300bhp, and the 330bhp six-cylinder Ferraris: who will ever forget the 'Grand Prix' start to that fateful Le Mans race, with Mike Hawthorn, Juan-Manuel Fangio and Eugenio Castelloti all involved? Rumours that Maserati was developing a new V8 racing engine (this would eventually appear, a 400bhp/4.5-litre layout, in 1956) then followed, finally convincing Jaguar that if they were to remain in world-class motor racing, then they needed a new and much more powerful engine.

Accordingly, when I arrived in the Jaguar design office as a junior designer in 1958, I was astonished to discover that a big new V12 engine had already been designed, though not yet built. By that time Jaguar had withdrawn from motor racing, which meant that the need to develop a V12 in a hurry had gone away, so the sheaf of drawings was put away. Bill Heynes's designers knew full well that they could not match Ferrari and Maserati with developments of the existing XK 'six', so if they seriously intended to return to sports car racing they would have to start again. The design team was still very small, and time was short, so there was no scope for a lengthy investigation of new layouts.

It therefore seemed logical to choose a V12 layout, and as far as I know, although other cylinder arrangements might have been seriously considered, none were ever built, even for testing. What was good enough for the Italians, surely, would be good enough for Jaguar.

By choosing a V12 engine arrangement and twin-cam cylinder heads, Jaguar saw a quick way to design a new layout that could use many proven XK components, including valve gear and camshafts. However, the rather limited space in the middle of a 60-degree V meant that entirely new cylinder heads, complete with downdraught inlet ports, would be needed.

Because this particular engine never progressed far beyond the scheme stage in the late 1950s, details are sparse, but it is worth remembering that a new short-stroke 2,483cc version of the XK engine had recently gone into production, and that doubling this would have given a 5-litre V12 capacity (actually 4,966cc), which would have been extremely useful for the new racing engine!

The 1960s

The whole idea of building a V12 engine then lay dormant until the early 1960s, when Jaguar once again began to dabble with the idea of returning to sports car racing. The earlier design was revisited, bore and stroke dimensions were altered, detail changes were made (especially with later experience in late-model D-Types and racing E-Type engines in mind), and component manufacture began in 1963. The very first V12 engine, a 5-litre engine with fuel injection and downdraught inlet pipes, ran on a testbed in August 1964.

It was no coincidence that this was also the year in which Ford sent prototypes of the GT40 to compete at Le Mans, and in which Bill Heynes authorized a start on the building of a new mid-engined XJ13 racing sports car. To match the Fords and the 400bhp 330P Ferraris, this car would need to be immensely powerful – so an efficient

new 5-litre V12 engine would be absolutely ideal for the job.

This is where the development sequence begins to get rather complicated. On the one hand, the V12 engine had been designed as a racing unit, and continued to be developed in that direction during 1965 and 1966. However, on the other hand Sir William Lyons and Bill Heynes could see the attraction of putting a series of ultra-powerful Jaguar cars into production.

At this time, there is no doubt that Jaguar considered – though did not always build – a whole variety of new engine layouts. In the early 1960s, well before the V12 design was resurrected, an entirely new and larger, twin-cam straight-six engine was schemed out – I have personal experience of this, for in my job as a junior designer I spent much time detailing the components which layout man John Waite had schemed out.

In the 1970s there was also the concept of turning the V12 into a complete family, including a V8 and even a V6, but little came of this. Sir William Lyons certainly consulted some of his most important dealer contacts about new engines. As one of them, North American entrepreneur Kjell Qvale, is reputed to have said:

> Sir William and I had a lot of chats and I gave him ideas. He asked me if he should make an eight or a twelve and I said to him that the world was full of eights …

Looked at from an American standpoint, this was certainly true, for every North American manufacturer already had its own brand of V8 on sale. In the mid-1960s some, like the 340bhp/7-litre Cadillacs, the 320bhp/7.6-litre Lincolns and the 360bhp/6.8-litre Chryslers were much more powerful than anything Jaguar had yet achieved, though we now know that many of the American horsepower claims were exaggerated.

In the end, the V12 was chosen for good, even compelling, technical reasons. As Jaguar's top engine designers, Walter Hassan and Harry Mundy, later commented in a promotional film made to introduce the engine in 1971:

Hassan: Well, we wanted to produce an engine that was outstanding. We wanted to sell quite a lot in America, so therefore we felt it should be something rather better than the run-of-the mill V8 engine in common usage over there. The twelve-cylinder was obviously a good choice. It has the technical excellence of extremely smooth running.

Mundy: By virtue of its inherent characteristics, there are no out-of-balance forces, either from a primary or secondary source. Except for its 60-degree V angle, and the basic architecture of the assembly, the V12 engine that eventually went into production at Radford in 1971 was completely different from the racing unit seen in the mid-engined XJ13. Not only did it have single-cam cylinder heads instead of the twin-cam heads with downdraught inlet ports of the XJ13, but it was also enlarged to 5,343cc by a bore increase. Cylinder heads and the cylinder block were both in cast aluminium.

With pending USA exhaust emission regulations in mind, instead of Lucas fuel injection, the first production engines were fuelled by four Zenith-Stromberg constant-vacuum carburettors (two for each bank).

Even so, the world's press was excited by the prospect of the launch of the first modern series-production V12 engine, so there was much comment when it first appeared in the Series III E-Type of 1971. In this form it was rated at 272bhp (DIN) at 5,850rpm, with peak torque of 304 lb/ft at 3,600rpm.

Of equal importance was its refinement. At the time, all the usual clichés – such as

balancing a coin on edge to see how long it would stand there before the vibration knocked it over – were wheeled out, and many favourable comments about its silence and smoothness followed.

As installed in the Series III E-Type, *Autocar* testers described it as:

Incredibly smooth and refined new engine … the engine is virtually silent. There is no chain whine, no induction roar and precious little exhaust throb … The engine really is like a dynamo under the bonnet, never faltering, never sounding rough and always providing a long sustained shove in the back … The mechanical refinement of the Jaguar engine is totally unmatched by any car regardless of its price or market niche …

The only problem, even in the relatively light, relatively small E-Type, was that this was clearly a thirsty engine, for testers rarely achieved better results than 16mpg (18l/100km). When the same engine was later installed in the bigger XJ12 that figure dropped to a truly awful 12mpg (24l/100km). In the USA, where gallons are smaller, the recorded figures were even lower – and in the case of the XJ12 it was even possibly to record worse than 10(US)mpg!

XJ27 INTO XJ-S – THE DEVELOPMENT PERIOD

By 1970 Sir William Lyons had decided to back the development of XJ27, a much larger and more luxurious car than the E-Type. In spite of the E-Type's fine reputation, it was no longer a very profitable model, for it took up too much of the space at Browns Lane for the sales and profit it brought in.

As part of his unadvertised rationalization plan, XJ27 would have to be based on the platform of the modern XJ6/XJ12, so that there could be production, technical and financial economies. British Leyland, his ultimate overlord, were happy to approve this, as they were already having to ration investment capital among their various plants.

Serious design work got under way in 1970; certainly by the time the Series III E-Type was launched, Jaguar had already decided not to develop a direct replacement. As ever, the first studies were of styling shapes, not only from aerodynamicist Malcolm Sayer's drawing board and computations, but in the secret styling department that Sir William Lyons visited every day.

Even at this stage, though, Sir William had to decide on the platform, suspensions and basic mechanical layout – the very basis of the car. Although it was easy enough to decide to base it on that of the XJ6/XJ12, should it be the same wheelbase or should it be shorter?

Since XJ27 was meant to be a generous 2+2 seater coupé, everyone seems to have agreed that the standard 108.8in (2,763mm) wheelbase was far too long. In the end it was decided to shorten the platform, in as simple a way as possible, and a wheelbase of 102.0in (2,591mm) was chosen – the shortest ever to be used on that basis.

It is instructive to compare the various Jaguar wheelbase dimensions of the period:

Wheelbase (in)	Origin	Models
102	XJ6	'XJ27' (XJ-S)
105	E-Type	E-Type SIII
108.8	XJ6	XJ6, XJ12, XJ Coupé
112.8	XJ6	XJ6L, XJ12L (and all later XJ6/XJ12 types)

The XJ27 project, therefore, was to have a shorter wheelbase than the obsolescent E-Type, though because the platform was wider and the packaging was not compromised by aerodynamic considerations, the XJ27 would have a larger and more capacious cabin.

Progress

In happier times – happier in human and financial terms – progress might have been faster and more assured, but at this time there were several serious hold-ups.

The first, tragically, was that Malcolm Sayer, who was so important to the shaping of high performance Jaguars, died suddenly – when he was only fifty-four years old. Sayer had already begun contributing to Sir William Lyons's styling ideas for XJ27 – the always controversial 'sail panels' (or 'flying buttresses') that linked the corners of the coupé roof to the rear wings were certainly his idea, for they provided a contribution to high-speed stability – and more was on the way.

It is no criticism to anyone else to point out that there was no one who could possibly replace Sayer. His methods were unique, his mathematical approach to shaping cars was never shared with his colleagues and – if I am honest – his preference for rounded styles was already going out of fashion, not only at Jaguar, but throughout the European motor industry.

The second factor affecting development was that Sir William Lyons decided to retire from executive management in March 1972. Although he was already seventy years of age he still looked amazingly trim, and was still a bustling and effective chairman. Sir William, though, decided that fifty years in the same business was enough, and made a clean break: except for making courtesy visits to 'his' old business, and being consulted about the style of future Jaguars, he was no longer involved in Jaguar's strategy. Functionally and financially, 'Lofty' England took over from Sir William, but there was really no one who could replace Jaguar's founder as a stylist/designer. Work on XJ27 had been going ahead for some time, but was by no means finalized, and although the basic lines were already there, much work had to be done to settle the details. Finally, though he made sure that the succession was assured by this time, Walter Hassan also chose to retire in April 1972. Hassan, the creator of the productionized V12 engine, handed over to his long-time friend and deputy, Harry Mundy.

Nevertheless, the basic shape of XJ27 *had* already been settled, and would finally be frozen before the end of 1972. Several of the styling 'cues' that became familiar on the XJ-S had all been tried out on prototypes and mock-ups in earlier years, as some of the pictures used in this book make clear.

The cut-off tail, for example, was really a refinement of the original XJ6 design, which had originally developed as a modification of the very E-Type-like styles that had been shaped in the mid-1960s. The move towards large ovoid headlamps (which would give way to twinned circular lamps for the USA market) had been evident in late 1960s styling studies, and would persist into the 1980s,

Another clay model of studies leading to the XJ-S shows two differing front-end treatments, one side with ovoid headlamp (quite close, in fact, to what was finally adopted), the other having a smaller grille but a large and unspecified place for headlamps.

eventually to be standardized on the original 'XJ40' (new-generation XJ6) saloon of 1986.

Although the XJ27 package had been settled by the spring of 1972 – in my final foray into industrial work, I was privileged to visit Jaguar's body development shops at this time, and saw full-size wooden mock-ups where seating, facias and instrument layouts were already being finalized – the style work still had to be settled.

By this time Bob Knight, who had been chief development engineer when the XJ6 was being designed (and who was personally renowned for the quite remarkable ride and refinement in that platform), had become Jaguar's technical director. From 1972, by

definition, he also took control of the still-small styling department.

Bob Knight recalls that he thought Sir William Lyons

> a natural stylist… he understood intuitively the fundamentals of styling, of line and light, since style is only perceived by virtue of reflected light; he had the most incredible flair for line.

Knight therefore had to carry on this process, using a small department headed by Doug Thorpe, along with other later-famous names like Oliver Winterbottom, Colin Holtum and George Thompson. Pictures of early

Shy, retiring, scholarly – Bob Knight has been described in so many ways. In every way, however, he was the father of the XJ-S, for it was his technical team which produced such a magnificently refined and capable car in the early 1970s. Bob himself was Jaguar's managing director from 1978 to 1980.

Original XJ-S prototypes – where are they now ?

Very few XJ-S prototypes were ever built. The very first car carried a K-plate, which means that Jaguar first registered it in 1971/1972. This is an extract from a factory list of 1978, which shows how early cars were allocated:

Registration No.	Transmission	Usage/Fate
EHP 377K	Manual	Barrier crash test 1975
OWK 335M	Automatic	Scrapped September 1975
GKV 637N	Manual	
GKV 638N	Manual	Sold in 1978.
GWK 409N	Manual	Accident/written off February 1977
Not Reg.	Automatic	Scrapped January 1977
PWK 524R	Automatic	Accident/written off April 1977
KHP 40N	Automatic	Durability endurance tests
NDU 402P	Automatic	Exhaust emission tests
LDU 862P	Automatic	Cooling/engine bay ducting development

Note that several early cars were fitted with manual transmission – yet very few such production cars were ever built, and the manual option was abandoned in 1979.

Bob Knight

When Bob Knight took over as Jaguar's technical chief in 1972, his daunting task was to replace Bill Heynes. It was typical of Knight that he never seemed to flinch from this, for he retained the same genial, patient, rather schoolmasterly manner until the day that he retired in 1980. By this time he had been Jaguar's managing director for two years, under the more enlightened regime introduced by Sir Michael Edwardes.

When starting his career, Knight worked for the Standard Motor Co. before joining Jaguar in 1944. By the 1950s he had already become Jaguar's chief development engineer, operating in what we would now think to be a ludicrously small and sparsely equipped department at Browns Lane. By that time, though, he had already figured strongly in the chassis design of the C-Type racing sports car, and in the next few years it was his fanatical attention to detail, especially with regard to ride quality and refinement, that made the Jaguar XJ6, XJ12 and XJ-S models so phenomenally quiet and capable.

After Bill Heynes retired in 1969, Bob Knight became director of vehicle engineering, working alongside Walter Hassan, who was in charge of all power unit work. Once Walter had successfully seen the magnificent V12 into production, he retired, so from 1972 Bob Knight was in total control.

In many ways the XJ-S was an ideal example of Knight's high standards and expectations. When developing an ultra-refined machine like the XJ6 or the XJ-S, he seemed to have infinite patience, and always tried to inculcate this into his colleagues. He would rather see a new model launch delayed than to have to approve something that, in his eyes, was not yet ready for sale.

My abiding memory of Bob Knight is of a polite and civilized man, who often seemed to have an amused expression, a half-smile on his face, who enjoyed the explanation and exposition of his job, and who would certainly have been at home in a lecture theatre. It was typical of his modesty that when I encountered him at Walter Hassan's ninetieth birthday celebrations – fifteen years after Knight had retired – he was amazed that anyone should still recognize him.

Don't be fooled by the 1965-vintage registration number – for this is an early-1970s style which would lead to the XJ-S shape. Some people always preferred the four-headlamp motif which was only regularly seen on USA-market XJ-S cars.

XJ27/XJ-S styling models do not seem to have survived but as we now know, by viewing the many pictures of early XJ40/XJ6 styles which have survived, this team was always wedded to the idea of using ovoid headlamps and a 'straight-through' wing crown line.

Since then, of course, the style of what became the XJ-S has always inspired great controversy – and widely conflicting views. Some so-called Jaguar enthusiasts who would not see beyond the end of their E-Type influenced noses, condemned it out of hand. Others liked it for its chunky shape and for its more practical packaging, while others wished its detailing – particularly

around the nose, and those prominent 'sail' panels – could have been more delicately carried out. (What is interesting, however, is that in later years prototype cars were built without the 'sail' panels, were resisted by Jaguar's marketing staff and also rejected by privileged Jaguar-owning customers who were also allowed to see the cars. The proof of the pudding?)

Later, when it became clear that the XJ-S style was aerodynamically better than the E-Type had ever been, the 'Sayer-knew-best' sect was stunned into silence. How could this be? Was this even credible? Surely the D-Type and E-Type shapes, which had been held up as wind-cheating paragons for so many years, could not be beaten by such a large and more 'craggy' car? The fact is that when Jaguar took measurements in the mid-1970s, the last of the Series III E-Type coupés had a drag coefficient (Cd) of 0.455, with a frontal area (A) of 17.8 sq ft (1.65sq m), whereas the new and larger XJ-S had a frontal area of 19.8sq ft (1.8sq m) and a much lower drag coefficient of 0.39.

When the XJ-S was launched to the press in the summer of 1975, I attended a meeting where the ever-precise Knight actually spelled out those figures for journalists to absorb. He was totally defiant about the new car's shape, was clearly proud of his team's achievement, and pointed out that a measure of the total drag – Cd × A – for the XJ-S was 7.72, compared with 8.10 for the last of the E-Types.

The new car, in fact, not only had a better shape, but in spite of its bulk was also a more efficient package and should therefore be faster – or, if that was the way an owner wanted to drive it, it should be a bit more economical than before.

By the end of 1972, therefore, the XJ27 style was signed off on its 102in (2,591mm) XJ6-derived platform, and serious design and development work could begin.

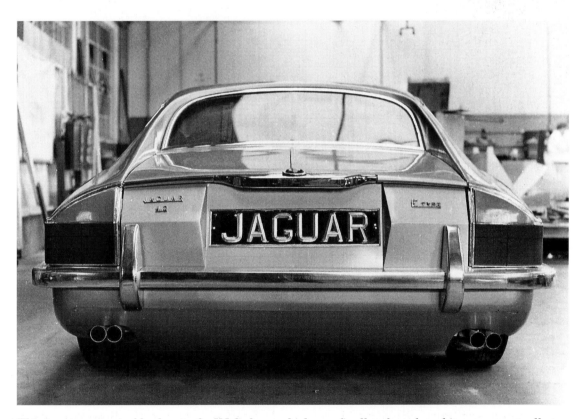

This is very recognizably close to the XJ-S shape which was finally adopted, and it appears actually to be a prototype, rather than a wood/clay mock-up. The significance, though, is in badging, which reads 'Jaguar 4.2' and 'E-Type' – yet the real XJ-S never used the XK engine, and was never to be called 'E-Type' either.

XJ-S style front ends were also tried out on four-door saloon mock-ups, too – this being one of many shapes tested in the 1970s on the way to finalization of the second-generation XJ6 (the 'XJ40') project.

XJ-S – WHAT SORT OF CHARACTER?

The biggest problem was not necessarily to settle a style, but to settle the car's character – and its title. Even though the choice of a 102in, 2+2 GT coupé had already been made, options were still available when it came to settling the 'tone' of the new machine. Not least of this was the question of the car's name.

Since sales in the North American market would be all-important to the new car's prospects, Graham Whitehead was involved at a very early stage. He recalls that although the car's character was very different from that of the E-Type, that was what the market place seemed to want.

Even though this was to be a totally different type of sporting Jaguar, there was certainly a groundswell of opinion that thought the new car should be called the F-Type, or XK-F. John Dugdale, an ex-*The Autocar* staff writer who became Jaguar's publicity manager in the 1960s and 1970s, recalls in his book *Jaguar in America* that:

As I recall, Bob Burden, then national advertising manager [in the USA] wanted XKF, or perhaps F-Type. Andrew Whyte, in charge of public relations at the Browns Lane factory, was dismayed, pointing out that XK was the six-cylinder engine series. In the USA the public had long continued to insist on calling the E-Type the XKE. We in the advertising world also liked this

Sneak preview for the Americans – this being John Dugdale's snap of a very early car, months before it was ready to go on sale in North America.

idea… XK meant a lot in North America after more than twenty years.

Everyone had his idea for a name. Andrew Whyte's was not too brilliant, being Le Mans Coupé, or some such … Wiser councils prevailed and the Jaguar was christened XJ-S, which now seems thoroughly suitable.

It was Bob Berry, hanging on precariously (precariously only because British Leyland had been nationalized and was in turmoil) who himself announced the name at the factory launch in June 1975: 'The car is called XJ-S', he said, 'XJ-dash-S.' That hyphen was probably a whim of Bob's alone, but we have never forgotten.

Mike Cook, who would have the job of helping to introduce the new car to the North American media, told me that there was a great deal of soul searching ahead of the new car:

When we saw the car before it was finalized, there was ambivalence. I don't think many people were enthusiastic, but I don't think anyone said it was terrible either. A lot of people actually said, 'What is it?' – because there was some doubt as to who we were going to sell this car to. Obviously it wasn't a pure sports car, but also obviously it was much more up-market than something like a Camaro or a Firebird.

49

The styling was a mixture, for it did not look like any previous Jaguar in any way, shape or form – inside or out. It was a complete departure.

This was typical of the stir caused by the advent of this completely new type of Jaguar, and naturally this also rubbed off to an extent on the engineers and designers who were finalizing the specification. For once, in fact, they had plenty of time to do this, as the launch of the car was somewhat held up by the long-drawn-out farewell given to the E-Type, by the turmoil in which British Leyland found itself in 1974, and by the need to rejig the facilities at Browns Lane to make way for the XJ-S.

Worse than all this, of course, was the cataclysm of the Energy Crisis, which exploded on the civilized world in October/November 1973. For Jaguar this could not have occurred at a worse time: an event that instantly made all large-engined, heavy, thirsty cars deeply unfashionable arrived when Jaguar had just frozen the design of its new XJ-S and committed millions of pounds to press tooling!

NEW MANAGEMENT, NEW IDEAS

After Sir William Lyons retired in March 1972, Lofty England became Jaguar's chairman and managing director. His first major new-model task was to see the V12-engined XJ12 safely into production (it did not help that this car was announced while the workforce was on strike, in a dispute over pay and conditions!), and his next was to oversee the launch of the longer-wheelbase Jaguar XJ6L and XJ12L models and their near-identical Daimler-badged equivalents.

These cars had a wheelbase and cabin 4in (100mm) longer than the standard car – all

that extra being devoted to rear seat space – and were much more highly priced than before. At the time my good friends on *Autocar* magazine commented that 'Daimler Vanden Plas motoring costs £400 an inch more than the standard car'.

Meanwhile, work was going ahead on the next phase of XJ6/XJ12 engineering, which would directly benefit the forthcoming XJ-S. Principally, with an eye to improving the V12 engine's power and exhaust emission efficiency, electronic Bosch-Lucas fuel injection took over from the original four-Zenith-Stromberg carburettor installation.

Although the system was basically a German Bosch design, Lucas had a considerable involvement in the Jaguar layout, quite simply because the Bosch unit was originally only capable of triggering eight injectors and had to be redeveloped to deal with twelve cylinders.

By modifying the V12 engine in this way, Jaguar not only improved peak power by 12.6 per cent and peak torque by 10.5 per cent, but also promised slightly better fuel efficiency. As a bonus, the massive fuel-injected engine looked somewhat tidier than the original type had ever been, though there was still a daunting collection of manifolds, pipes, electrical leads, fuel injection components and ancillaries inside the centre of the vee.

Once this new derivative of the engine had been developed, the mechanical specification of the XJ-S fell rapidly into place. Except that the E-Type's four-speed manual gearbox was to be offered as a transmission option (there was no manual transmission XJ12), the entire running gear and chassis was basically that of the XJ12, for the V12 engine was to be in exactly the same state of tune. However, to take account of the XJ-S's smaller size and probable higher top speed, the back axle ratio was raised from 3.31:1 to 3.07:1.

WHERE TO BUILD THE CARS?

Then, in 1973, there was another management upheaval. At a critical moment, when the XJ-S was being committed to series production, British Leyland moved to appoint a thirty-four-year-old economist, Geoffrey Robinson, as Jaguar's managing director. Robinson, who had already been British Leyland's financial controller, and recently been running the Innocenti subsidiary in Italy, was obviously the 'new broom':

> Lofty was soon due to retire, so Donald Stokes brought me in as managing director. The philosophy was to keep Jaguar largely as an autonomous unit: I was thoroughly committed to the motor industry and British Leyland – who could want a better company to run than Jaguar?

Geoffrey Robinson was drafted in by Lord Stokes as Jaguar's Managing Director in the autumn of 1973, also becoming Chairman in 1974 when 'Lofty' England retired. Robinson's strategy envisaged considerable expansion, the rationalization of assembly lines to accept the XJ-S being an important factor. Having fought unsuccessfully against the entire premise of the Ryder 'rescue' plan, he left the company in 1975.

Frank Raymond Wilton ('Lofty') England (1922–95)

Although 'Lofty' – few other than Sir William Lyons ever called him anything else! – is more famous as Jaguar's motorsport team manager, he was also an important executive at Jaguar through the 'Big Jaguar' years. When the 3.5-litre was at its height he was the company's service manager, and by the time the last 420G of all was produced, he had become Jaguar's joint managing director.

Born and educated in London, 'Lofty' was then apprenticed to Daimler's depot in Hendon as an engineer, where he soon acquired his nickname as a recognition of his tall figure. Having become a racing mechanic to, among others, Sir Henry 'Tim' Birkin, Whitney Straight, Dick Seaman and Prince Birabongse Bhanuban ('B.Bira'), he later joined Alvis, of Coventry, as a service engineer.

After serving as a Lancaster pilot with the RAF during World War Two (a brave man's job which he rarely discussed), he returned to Alvis, then became Jaguar's service manager in 1946. During the 1950s he combined this job with that of competitions manager, presiding over victories at Le Mans in 1951, 1953 and 1955.

From 1956 'Lofty' became service director, and had to withdraw from active involvement in motor sport, for he then began to move inexorably up the management ladder. In 1961 (the year in which the Mark X was introduced) he became assistant managing director, in 1966 he was appointed deputy managing director (the year in which Jaguar joined hands with BMC), then in 1967 Sir William Lyons made him his joint managing director, a position he retained for years after Jaguar was absorbed into British Leyland.

Throughout the 1950s and 1960s, therefore, 'Lofty' was a party to every decision made regarding new Jaguars. When Sir William stepped down in 1972, 'Lofty' became Jaguar's chief executive, but held this position for less than two years before retiring.

He soon moved to a retirement home in Austria with his second wife. Although that was the end of his active involvement in business, he remained fiercely loyal to Jaguar, its image and its heritage. Though living far away from Great Britain, he kept closely in touch with every motoring development. Motoring writers like me soon learned to check and double-check all Jaguar material written, for woe-betide any of us who made mistakes – the admonitory letter would soon arrive!

Jaguar was always profitable, a real cash generator, right through this period, but the situation would get very difficult after that first oil price rise.

Even by this time, John Barber (Lord Stokes's deputy) had instituted a five-year planning cycle, which we worked up, incorporating facelifts, and the first all-new car was to be the XJ-S. We costed it carefully, made our presentation, and the word came back that this plan looked terrifically good for Jaguar.

In a matter of months Lofty England decided to retire, leaving Robinson in sole charge at Jaguar. Robinson admits:

It wasn't an easy relationship with Lofty. I was trying to do new things. I always liked Lofty, personally, and we became quite good friends. However, towards the end of his life I know he wasn't always as complimentary about me as I always was about him. Certainly I always wanted the best possible working relationship with him, but his was a non-executive post, it was titular. In addition to the natural friction between young guard and old guard, I think he found that rather annoying.

Robinson buckled down to pushing through the major changes needed at Browns Lane:

When I arrived there were no plans to increase production, though the demand was there. I think that part of my brief was that we had to increase capacity, and to produce cars more in line with demand.

The XJ-S was a key factor. It was a modern car, a new car, and the sales projections were a bit higher than for the E-Type. More important was the forecast that the XJ-S was always likely to be a very profitable car.

But we had to get the E-Type out of the plant before we could lay down tracks for the XJ-S, for otherwise we couldn't build the new car. The plans were to lengthen the existing two tracks.

At Browns Lane, simply, there was the fact that the assembly tracks weren't anywhere near long enough. The cars were more complicated and bigger than previous models, and needed more space. Even then, it wasn't possible to get more than 50,000 cars a year out of the plant.

And so it was that the XJ-S moved slowly, sometimes painfully, towards public launch. Naturally the contract for producing body monocoques went to Pressed Steel Fisher

In the 1970s and 1980s the XJ-S was always an important part of the scene at Browns Lane, but it was Jaguar (and Daimler) saloons like these which sold in the largest numbers. These cars, in fact, are late-model V12-engined cars, which shared the same engine, transmission and running gear with the XJ-S of the period.

(another British Leyland subsidiary), who elected to build them at the old 'Fisher & Ludlow' plant at the Castle Bromwich plant on the eastern outskirts of Birmingham. This was one of Jaguar's earliest links with Castle Bromwich, a complex that later became part of the privatized Jaguar empire.

Engines and manual gearboxes would come from Jaguar's Radford factory, automatic transmissions came from Borg Warner, and rear axles from Salisbury, while final assembly would be on a dedicated line at the much-modified Browns Lane premises. But it was not easy, as Geoffrey Robinson remembers:

When the XJ-S was first put into pilot production there were a hell of a lot of production problems, particularly around the facia, which was a murderous thing to fit.

Ready at last! This was the XJ-S as finally revealed in 1975: larger, faster, more wind-cheating, but certainly more controversial in style than the last of the E-Types.

Pressed Steel Co. Ltd (later Pressed Steel Fisher Ltd)

Starting with the Mark VII model, Jaguar sourced all their saloon car body shells – whether separate or unit-construction types – from the Pressed Steel Co. Ltd, originally from Cowley, near Oxford, and later from Castle Bromwich, east of Birmingham.

Originally founded in 1926 as a joint venture between Morris Motors and the Edward G. Budd Manufacturing Co. of the USA, Pressed Steel specialized in building welded-together all-steel bodies, all its initial supplies going to Morris. However, because of this obvious financial and geographical link with Morris, Pressed Steel found it difficult to gain orders from other car-makers, the result being that Morris pragmatically sold out their shareholding in 1930. Thereafter Pressed Steel expanded rapidly, and by the end of the 1930s were doing business with every member of British 'Big Six' car makers.

SS Cars, later Jaguar Cars, originally took some pressings towards building their own shells, but for the Mark VII it was decided to source the entire shell, still in what the industry quaintly called the 'body in white' (unpainted) state, from a specialist. Mark VII shells were soon joined by monocoque 2.4/3.4-litre shells, and the largest Jaguar of all, the Mark X, took over in 1961.

By this time Pressed Steel were very large indeed, for in addition to Jaguar they were also supplying BMC, Rootes, Rolls-Royce, Rover, Standard-Triumph and Daimler with shells. When they were taken over by BMC in 1965, Jaguar had doubts about the security of future supplies, but after Jaguar also joined forces with BMC that concern evaporated.

After the foundation of British Leyland, Pressed Steel became subsumed into Pressed Steel Fisher, but Jaguar continued to take body shell supplies for many years until they developed their own body plant at Castle Bromwich in the 1980s. The Jaguar XJ-S, in fact, was always supplied from Castle Bromwich, where it was pressed and assembled throughout its long career.

I remember going down to the track and finding a track worker with his knuckles red raw in trying to fit this damned facia. I also recall several instances of fouls occurring, where one part couldn't be fitted to the other. Bob Knight's team's drawings were OK, the suppliers just weren't making parts correctly 'to drawing'.

There were other problems. It wasn't the easiest car to build. I think that most Jaguars at the time were very difficult to get into production. Engineering resources were very limited – probably too small, honestly, to bring in major new models.

All this, compounded by British Leyland's highly publicized financial problems, meant that the XJ-S could not possibly have appeared at a more difficult time. But there is an inertia, an impetus, behind the arrival of a major new model that cannot be stopped. Once the tooling is complete, orders are placed, once the parts start coming in, the cars have to be built, and before long advertising strategies, previews and launches follow up.

Even at the beginning of 1975, when some doom-mongers did not think that British Leyland could possibly survive, the XJ-S rolled inexorably towards announcement. By September, whatever had happened to British Leyland in the interim, the XJ-S would be ready to go on sale.

How would it be received?

4 XJ-S on Sale: 1975 to 1981

Although the E-type had dropped out of production in September 1974, Jaguar actually held back the news until the end of February 1975. Naturally this encouraged the flow of maudlin tidal waves of comment from motoring writers and enthusiasts all round the world, much of it suggesting that the E-Type had been murdered rather than allowed to fade peacefully away.

The scene was now set for the new car – XJ-S – to appear, though this could not possibly have happened at a worse time. Not only was the world still struggling to escape from the Energy Crisis, which had resulted in colossal increases in oil prices, but even among wealthy drivers this state of affairs had made big and thirsty engines like the V12 most unpopular.

Add to this the fact that Jaguar's owners, British Leyland, had recently and most publicly had to be financially rescued, then nationalized, by the government. Also, that the E-Type fraternity were most publicly doubting if a replacement could be as good, and it is clear that the months leading up to the arrival of XJ-S could not have been less favourable.

PRELUDE

Jaguar moved swiftly to condition the world for the new car. As *Autocar* commented in March, when giving the E-Type its requiem:

It is clear that the E-Type's replacement, scheduled for later this year, will be a closed coupé rather than a rugged wind-in-the-hair two seater.

In the American subsidiary's valedictory press release, Graham Whitehead (whose then-title was president, British Leyland Motors Inc.) commented that:

We are not taking Jaguar out of the sports car field. A new and different type of sports model will be announced later this year.

Nevertheless, the first half of 1975 was a turbulent period for Jaguar – in fact for everyone connected with British Leyland. Following the financial collapse came the Ryder Report, then in the spring came rescue by the injection of huge amounts of capital. British Leyland was thus effectively nationalized, thereafter being controlled by the National Enterprise Board.

At the same time, structural and financial upheaval was threatened, for Sir Don Ryder's report (which was adopted by the government) proposed total rationalization of Leyland's car-making businesses into one conglomerate – and with it a total loss of Jaguar identity. Jaguar's young chairman, Geoffrey Robinson, was appalled at the prospect:

The question was, which way forward for the company as a whole? We fought very

Side view of the first-generation XJ-S, showing that it was a longer and rather bulkier shape than the E-Type. Technically, though, Jaguar had made great strides, for not only did this car have a bigger cabin and a lot more accommodation than the E-Type, but it also had a lower drag coefficient. North American versions – this is one – had a tiny badge close to the fuel filler cap which reminded owners to use unleaded fuel. The first British price was £8,900, the first North American price $19,200.

strenuously, not really to keep Jaguar on its own – that was no longer a practical proposition – but we put forward a new proposal which pointed out that Jaguar was now too small to stay on its own, Rover was too small on its own, and Triumph was too small on its own.

What we needed to do was to integrate those three businesses into a specialist car company, like BMW. You would have had a marvellous range, and we even drew up plans of how the product and the facilities could be rationalized and integrated.

This, in fact, was my proposal, at least four years before Jaguar-Rover-Triumph was formed. There was resistance to my proposal, not from within Jaguar, but from the Ryder team, who produced what I called the 'Ford solution', the full-scale forced integration.

Jaguar people, in general, perceived that the 'JRT solution' was the best hope for their future in 1975. Most people saw it as a very practical move forward, which would work. At the time we had positive cash flow and profits, and we could certainly have gone on, on our own, as Jaguar – for a while but not permanently. I don't believe that Jaguar could have carried on indefinitely without a partner, somewhere.

But Robinson's lobbying was in vain:

My JRT proposal was turned down in favour of an integrated automotive division. Donald Stokes said, 'Well, you realize, Geoffrey, that Jaguar will cease to exist?', then told me he wanted me to do a bigger job in the new division, but never specified what. I don't think they would have let me have the top job – and I wouldn't have accepted it because I didn't believe it could be done.

I said that I was not interested in a new integrated system, said that I thought it was the wrong way to go, and argued our case for JRT.

For a few weeks, therefore, Robinson was the classic corporate 'lame duck', but eventually resigned:

I walked out because Jaguar, as a business, ceased to exist. You had a managing director of Leyland Cars, Derek Whittaker, but Browns Lane just became part of the 'Body and Assembly Division'. Radford – well! Radford then reported in to the managing director of the Power Train Division. Parts were controlled somewhere else.

Although a modified JRT business would eventually be set up at the end of the decade (after Sir Michael Edwardes took control of British Leyland), it was a rather different operation. Geoffrey Robinson faded rapidly out of the Jaguar picture in the spring of 1975, then after a few months revived his close interest in politics by becoming the Member of Parliament for the Coventry North-West constituency – which just happened to include Jaguar within its boundaries:

I kept well away from British Leyland politics after that, because it was very embarrassing to me. What I made clear to the management was that as an MP I would do anything possible to support them, because a lot of my constituents worked there.

PRE-PRODUCTION

One of Geoffrey Robinson's major achievements had been to oversee the shake-up of the assembly lines and layout at Browns Lane:

When I arrived, there were no plans to increase production, and I think it's fair to say that the thinking of Sir William, then Lofty, was to keep production fairly tight, and to keep it to the order book if they could.

But when I arrived – this was before the Energy Crisis, of course – we had a 2½-year order book, with Jaguars in terrific demand throughout the world, and we could sell more motor cars than we had been planning to build.

There was another aspect, that the Jaguar factory was so tight – physically tight – in production facilities, that the quality of the product was suffering. The first thing we did, therefore, was to lengthen the tracks, to give more track space, to give more room and easier access around the cars. As part of the strategy, we also planned to bring in a new paint plant: the paint system was very antiquated.

The levels we were looking at were to go up to a comfortable 50,000 or 60,000 cars a year, all of the XJ6 and XJ-S type. We could get this much out of Browns Lane, but it wasn't possible to have more than one basic model.

This, Robinson insists, was one of the factors behind the decision to drop the E-Type well before the XJ-S was ready to go into production. However, the fact that in the aftermath of the Energy Crisis (and because it was

Geoffrey Robinson (born 1939)

After Sir William Lyons had retired, and after Lofty England felt obliged to take early retirement, the next Jaguar chairman was always likely to be faced with 'Mission Impossible'. Geoffrey Robinson not only tackled this challenge with relish, but aimed to double Jaguar's rate of production during his tenure.

Born in Sheffield, Geoffrey Robinson studied German and Russian at Cambridge University, then gained a fellowship to Yale to read economics before returning to England in 1964.

For the next four years, he worked in the Labour Party's research organisation, then joined the Industrial Reorganization Corporation at a time when it was heavily involved in encouraging a merger between Leyland and BMH (which included Jaguar). Immediately after the 1970 general election the IRC was closed down, whereupon Robinson joined British Leyland, and soon became Financial Controller. After he had run the negotiations to buy Innocenti, he was sent out to Italy by Lord Stokes to manage that business.

Only eighteen months later, Lord Stokes called him back to the UK and installed him as Jaguar's managing director and chief executive, immediately under 'Lofty' England, who was chairman. He was then only thirty-four, and had only been in direct contact with the motor industry for three years. The vastly more experienced England stayed on for just four months under this Stokes-inspired regime before electing to retire, whereupon Robinson became Jaguar's chairman. Although this move occurred during the depths of the first Energy Crisis, the enthusiastic Yorkshireman immediately laid plans to double Jaguar's production capability – to 60,000 cars a year – and pushed ahead with the implementation of the complex XJ6/XJ12 Series II programme, which included the two-door XJ coupés, the Vanden Plas derivatives of the latest Daimlers, and the completion of the new short-wheelbase XJ-S project.

In retrospect, this period is now seen as a time of great turmoil at Jaguar, where many middle and senior managers were demonstrably unhappy. They must have become even more unhappy in the early months of 1975, after British Leyland had been taken into state ownership, and after the Ryder Report offered a quite impossibly optimistic vision of the corporation's future.

The Ryder Report proposed that Jaguar should be completely amalgamated into Leyland Cars, leaving no place for a separate and autonomous Jaguar chairman and chief executive. Because Geoffrey Robinson opposed this policy, he resigned, and left the industry of which he had been a member for only five years. Later, he became a Labour MP for the Coventry constituency that includes the Jaguar Browns Lane factory.

such an old-fashioned model by this time) it was proving hard to sell was also a factor:

The E-Type was never a 'nuisance', and I was always delighted to have it there. But when it became clear that we couldn't accommodate it with the other expansion plans, along with the arrival of the XJ-S to supersede it, we had to take a decision.

I ran out the E-Type to make space for the XJ-S – but we knew we had this wonderful, historic car, and I wanted all the

tooling to be preserved, so that at any time we could pick up the preserved tooling, and reproduce cars. I certainly had it all bonded for a time, but I don't know what happened after I left.

If the XJ-S had been fully developed at the time, perhaps it could have been made ready some months earlier, but there was no way that it could be put on sale until the assembly lines at Browns Lane had been rearranged, and the pre-production problems sorted out.

59

Although this publicity picture is carefully shot to make the rear compartment look larger, in fairness it was much more spacious than that of the E-Type. But it helped to have short legs...

It would, in any case, have been unwise to rush it on to the market place. Not only would the first export cars have arrived in North America at the wrong time of the year, but the launch would also have interfered with the arrival of the two-door Jaguar coupés and the new XJ3.4 model, all of which were actually launched in May 1975.

LAUNCH IN TWO CONTINENTS

After several months of rumour and counter-rumour, the XJ-S was officially revealed in September 1975, though Jaguar dealers had been given a preview as early as January. Looking back now, though, it is a miracle that the new car ever made it to the showrooms at all, as Jaguar without Geoffrey Robinson no longer seemed to have a top man.

By this time Jaguar, as a company, had virtually ceased to exist – all this being part of the master plan laid out by Sir Don Ryder. To run the business (in theory at least), Cowley manufacturing specialist Tony Thompson was made chairman of a 'Jaguar operating committee', but there was little evidence of this ever having influence at Browns Lane.

The XJ-S's head-on aspect shows up the wide but shallow grille, and the large headlamps – oval for most markets, but four circular lamps for sale in the USA.

Without the sterling – stubborn, even – efforts of plant director Peter Craig (a long-time, died-in-the-wool, Jaguar man) and technical director Bob Knight, the business would have drifted further into oblivion. Jaguar's engineering king-pin, Knight always insisted in reporting direct to Derek Whittaker (not to an anonymous 'operating committee'!). Before the end of 1975, therefore, Knight had effectively become Jaguar's managing director – quite unofficially, and without status, of course – and it was he who led the launch team in the UK.

John Dugdale, who led the British Ley-land-USA publicity effort, has perfectly

When the XJ-S was launched, one-time chairman 'Lofty' England and ex-F1 motor-racing champion Phil Hill (from the USA) got together to admire one of the early cars:.Hill was much involved in the making of a promotional film about the new car.

summed up the approach to the launch of the XJ-S:

> The task... was to make a careful presentation to tell the true story behind the many engineering refinements that represent a new Jaguar. Also we suspected in advance that the XJ-S Coupé could be a disappointment to press, to owners, and to enthusiasts generally, who thirsted for an exotic new sports car.

This was a theme to which Jaguar would return again and again in 1975 – the XJ-S was a new sporting Jaguar, but it was not meant to replace the E-Type. The message was that nothing could do that – for this was

the mid-1970s, not the early 1960s, where the world of motoring, and Jaguar, had moved on a lot. Bob Knight summarized this perfectly in his presentations to the press:

> When the time came to consider the next sporting type of car (I say that rather than to say a successor to the E-Type), we were somewhat uncertain as to which direction to go at the outset since the E-Type had been a car of a very particular character... the market feel was that there was a wider market for the sophisticated 2+2 type configuration. So therefore we looked at the success which we had achieved at that time with the XJ6, and decided to build into a 2+2 the most attractive characteristics of

the XJ6 plus some others which would appeal to the more sporting type of driver.

This, in fact, was only one – probably the most important one – of a series of new product introductions that Jaguar carried out during 1975. First there had been the introduction of the XJC Coupé models (with a choice of six-cylinder and fuel-injected V12 engines), which had been previewed in late 1973, then the arrival of the first fuel-injected XJ12 saloons, followed by the launch of the XJ3.4 – an XJ6 saloon fitted with the 'traditional' Jaguar XK engine of 3,442cc capacity.

In the UK, the XJ-S was revealed to the press in a series of restrained technical and marketing appraisals chaired by Bob Knight, the journalists then getting the opportunity to hustle a handful of pre-production cars around the Cotswolds. Most of the available cars had automatic transmission, but it was typical of British journalists' sentiments than manual transmission was in great demand.

For me, that day was memorable for the pace at which this big car – and, make no mistake, it *was* a big car – could be thrust along the winding roads in the Cotswolds. I really only appreciated how fast when the back end suddenly twitched on a tight junction, for it needed good traction, a limited-slip differential, finger-light power steering and a modicum of good fortune to allow me to gather it all up again!

The USA-market launch actually began in June 1975, when writers from the prestigious monthly magazines were flown to the UK to hear Derek Whittaker talk about 'A Brave New World... for British Leyland'. Later, in August, the American ex-F1 World Champion, Phil Hill, flew to Coventry to help make a TV programme for transmission in the USA.

Finally, in September, early USA-specification cars, complete with quadruple head-lamps, less powerful engines, and all the compulsory extra equipment needed to meet fast-burgeoning crash and safety regulations, were finally ready for launch in North America. Because Jaguar originally hoped to sell well over half of XJ-S production to North America (that figure was certainly not achieved at first, but was achieved in the late 1980s and 1990s when a soft-top version finally came onto the scene) these were critical times – so cars were made available near Detroit (on the Belle Isle island in the middle of the river, where Indycar races were later promoted), then at Long Beach (close to Los Angeles) on the west coast.

Jaguar Cars Inc. (of the USA)

Without the sales achieved in North America, I doubt if Jaguar could ever have made any money from their sports cars, and certainly not from the XJ-S, which might also have meant that they could not have produced such successful saloons. In the 1990s, as in the 1950s, Jaguar relied on their USA sales to a great degree.

The first post-war Jaguars – 3.5-litre models – were sent to the USA in 1947, when Max Hoffman began selling cars on the east coast. Chuck Hornburg soon undertook a similar task on the west coast. Then, in 1952, Johannes Eerdmans arrived in the USA, later to direct Jaguar's transatlantic sales until he retired in 1971. Jaguar Cars North American Corporation was set up in 1954, becoming Jaguar Cars Inc. in 1958.

Although the majority of North American sales went to the sports cars at first, American buyers soon came to love the large and graceful saloons and coupés well. When the XJ-S was being developed, it was always clear that it was aimed squarely at North American preferences, as its sales over the years proved so strongly.

63

THE PRODUCT – IN DETAIL

As expected, there was controversy over the car's style, coupled with enormous interest in the technicalities. Even those analysts who had wanted to see a direct replacement for the E-Type were fascinated by the technical detail of the new XJ-S.

The structure, based on a short-wheel-base version of the XJ12 platform, was familiar enough, though in the development process much of the common engineering of the underside had actually been lost. Like most two-door coupés, it was torsionally stiffer than the four-door saloon on which it was based, and there is little doubt that the 'sail panels' on the rear quarters added a little to that rigidity.

At the front, a pair of Menasco struts (filled with a silicon-based plastic material that gradually recovered its shape after being compressed) were fitted behind the bumpers, to deal with the mandatory 5mph (8km/h) USA crash test, and there were side-intrusion resistant bars inside the doors that were connected to the hinges.

The most controversial XJ-S view of all, showing off the 'sail panels' (or 'flying buttresses') linking the roof with the tail of the car. These panels had an aerodynamic function, to aid stability – and when Jaguar test marketed cars without them, they found that observers actually liked them. This USA-market car has the large impact-absorbing bumpers made necessary by recent legislation.

The front-end detail was rather fussy on USA-market cars, for not only were there four headlamps, but side-repeater indicator lamps were also compulsory. The big energy-absorbing bumpers and the front spoiler would soon become familiar to Jaguar buyers.

All this, along with extra triangulation in the engine bay, and subtle other stiffening, meant that the shell weighed 720lb (327kg). This was at least 100lb (45kg) less than the current XJ12 saloon shell, but Jaguar thought it could have saved at least another 100lb (45kg) if the compulsory strengthening had not been in place.

There was a different layout from the XJ12 in the boot, for the familiar twin fuel tanks (one in each wing, at the corners) had been discarded in favour of a single tank across the front of the boot, above the rear suspension area. (This was another reason for the demise of the E-Type, incidentally: its rear-mounted under-floor tank could not possibly have remained in one piece after a compulsory 30mph (48km/h) rear crash test, which was due to apply to 1976 model-year cars.)

All in all, the XJ-S weighed about 3,900lb (1,770kg), which compared well with the 4,116lb (1,871kg) quoted for the current XJ12, this reduction allowing Bob Knight's development engineers to reduce (that is, soften) front and rear spring rates, while keeping careful control of the ride and the damping. Other minor suspension tweaks included the addition of a rear anti-roll bar – ahead of and below the line of the rear axle's drive shafts – and a higher front castor angle.

In general, however, the running gear of the XJ-S was virtually the same as that of the current XJ12, which is to say that the fuel-injected 5.3-litre V12 engine produced 285bhp (though at first the Californian-specification cars – not the other USA-spec. types – produced only about 244bhp: this short-fall would gradually be eroded in the years which followed), the automatic transmission was a three-speed Borg-Warner Model 12, and the Salisbury back axle carried a Powr-Lok limited slip differential with a 3.07:1 final drive ratio (3.31:1 for the lower-powered USA-market cars).

There was, however, one important difference –the E-Type's old-style four-speed all-synchromesh manual gearbox was available as a no-cost option to buyers outside the USA. This, in fairness, was no more than a sop to the traditionalists, as the manual box was at the very limit of its torque capabilities when matched to the 285bhp V12 engine.

As almost everyone except the die-hards had forecast, sales of manual-transmission XJ-Ss would always be very limited. No more than 352 such cars would ever be built as these figures confirm:

XJ-S – manual transmission production

1975	4
1976	130
1977	143
1978	63
1979	12

No nonsense screen/wiper/air inlet detailing on the early cars – concealed wipers would not arrive in Europe for many more years.

Jaguar's first fuel-injected 5.3-litre V12 engine was introduced in April 1975 for the latest Jaguar and Daimler saloons. The same unit went into the XJ-S, which was launched only months later.

In peak production (1977), manual-gearbox cars represented a mere 3.7 per cent of all XJ-S production. Once the XJ-S inherited a new type of GM automatic transmission in 1977, demand fell still further, and the option was finally dropped in 1979, the last regular (as opposed to special-order) car having been built in September.

It is now well known, of course, that Harry Mundy (who had become Jaguar's engine/transmission design chief when Walter Hassan retired) had already had a brand-new five-speed all-synchromesh manual transmission designed for use in modern Jaguars, and had seen several prototypes built, but was never able to push this feature through to production. This new transmission was apparently too large and too heavy to appeal to British Leyland's planners. It was typical of the irrepressible Mundy that he always went out of his way to talk about 'his' new gearbox, especially after BL forced Jaguar to take up the five-speed Rover-Triumph five-speeder in later years, quite against their will!

The most startling of innovations was reserved for the cabin, where there was not a square inch of wood veneer in sight. For Jaguar, this was an extraordinary omission, but was merely continuing the trend set in the E-Type. Jaguar, it seemed, were making an unspoken comment at this time – that

(Opposite, top)
Front suspension assembly at Jaguar's Radford
factory where the V12 engine and (until 1979)
the four-speed all-synchromesh manual gearbox
were also manufactured.

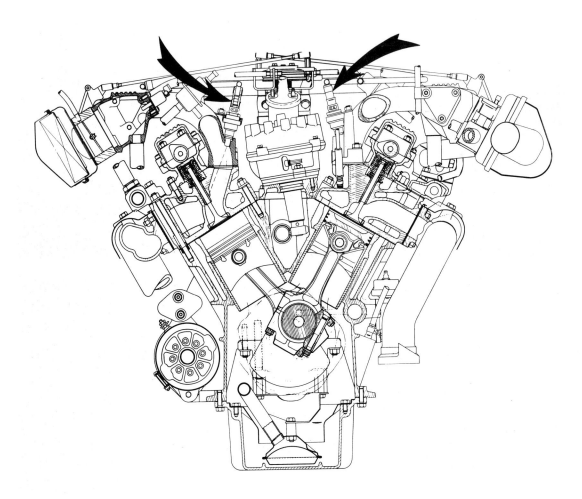

(Above)
This cross-section shows the general layout of the magnificent fuel-injected 5.3-litre V12 engine.
The arrows are pointing at the fuel injector nozzles which fired a spray of fuel towards the back of
the inlet valves.

(Opposite)
Room, but only just, for the V12 engine and all its ancillaries to fit into the engine bay of the XJ-S.
Maintenance? Not for the faint-hearted!

their saloons and limousines could have much wood veneer on the facia, and as door cappings, but that wood was considered old-fashioned and inappropriate for their sporting cars.

Jaguar managers, incidentally, might have been sure of themselves in this matter, but the customers clearly did not agree with them, and the muttering began almost at once. Jaguar would eventually heed them, and the first time the car was facelifted – for the HE model of 1981 – the wood duly reappeared. By 1996, when the XK8 was launched, there was no further misreading of sentiment, for wood was present in the new style from the start.

Although the dashboard was a complex one-piece vacuum-formed piece of plastic, the facia/instrument layout of the original XJ-S was a mixture of tradition and innovation, established XJ6/XJ12 components and new fittings. The traditional circular speedometer and rev-counter dials were placed at each side of vertical-drum minor dials, and although XJ6/XJ12-style switches and steering column controls were used, there was a proper handbrake lever (instead of the XJ6/XJ12 'umbrella' handle), which was mounted outboard of the driver's seat.

After being operated, incidentally, the handbrake lever flopped back to sill level, which made novices think that the linkage had failed the first time it had been tensioned! Not so – this was done merely to keep the lever handle well out of the driver's way when he swung his legs into the car from outside.

Reception

The first production cars were rolling down the assembly lines at Browns Lane at the same time as the car was unveiled. Deliveries to export markets – most particularly to the USA – would begin as soon as the shipping 'pipeline' could be filled. In fact the records show that 1,245 cars were built in 1975 (almost all of them in the last four

The original XJ-S's instrument panel was quite unlike that of earlier Jaguars, for there was a complete lack of wood, and the auxiliary instruments were laid out 'drum-style' in the main panel. Note the steering wheel style – no sign of bulky air bags in the 1970s!

months of the year), with 287 being sold in the USA before the end of December.

When the car was launched, Jaguar forecast that they would build about sixty XJ-S cars every week – which would equate to about 3,000 cars a year – though this was only the beginning. But was this enough – and had the effort been worth while? For comparison, E-Type production had once peaked at 170 cars a week, and in its last full year (1973) 4,686 cars were produced, or an average of ninety cars a week.

Jaguar's publicists had no doubt. In full-page colour advertisements published at the time of launch, a red XJ-S loomed under the magnificent headline, 'SEPTEMBER 10, 1975. A BLACK DAY FOR MODENA, STUTTGART AND TURIN', but perhaps there was a note of caution in the final sentence, tucked down at bottom right: 'The car everyone dreams of. But very, very few can ever own.'

Ignoring the tortured grammar for a moment, it is clear that this was an attempt to talk up the new car's exclusivity, and at the same time to take a swipe at other marques, such as Mercedes-Benz, Ferrari, Maserati and even Fiat.

Jaguar realized that the established E-Type clientele were already alienated by the new car, but the company was (and remained) convinced that there was a bigger world market for the larger, plusher, more saloon-like XJ-S model. The original aim, to sell 3,000 to 4,000 cars a year, was soon achieved, and for those who think this is a restricted figure, let me remind you that in the late 1970s Mercedes-Benz was only making about 6,000/7,000 a year of the SLC model – and that this car was available with a choice of three different engines, one of them an economy-conscious 2.8-litre 'six'.

As soon as it went on sale in the UK at an all-in price of £8,900, it was clear that the XJ-S could not possibly take the place of the E-Type, for it was in a completely different price bracket. It was, in fact, hugely more expensive than the last of the E-Types, which had retailed for a mere £3,743, though it compared well with the £11,271 demanded by Mercedes-Benz for the current 450SLC.

Testers' Opinions

To get it off the mark with a flourish, the XJ-S needed a series of laudatory road tests, and although it certainly got these in the UK, it was not quite so fulsomely received in North America.

Autocar, whose technical editor Jeff Daniels was a long-time Jaguar fan, greeted the car at launch with the headline 'A new concept in Jaguar motoring', and when its first full-length road test appeared in February 1976 (actually this car had manual transmission, which made it a real rarity) the XJ-S was described:

> as 'a great car' still cheaper than its international competition. A joy to drive...

The text was full of superlatives, and the statistics included a top speed of 153mph (246km/h), 0–60mph in 6.9sec, 0–100mph through the gears in 16.9sec and the standing ¼-mile sprint in 15.2sec, though all this was tempered by the overall fuel consumption of 15.4mpg (18.4l/100km), with the thought that this could fall below 14mpg (20l/100km) if the car was pushed really hard.

The most astonishing test of all was to start the car from rest in top (fourth gear), by switching off, pulling the car off the line on the starter motor, and letting the speed build up as soon as the magnificent V12 engine fired up and began to chug away! From that point, uncomplainingly and completely smoothly from about 4mph (6km/h), the car surged up to 140mph (225km/h) in just 70

Jaguar XJ-S 5.3-Litre (1975–81)

Layout
Unit-construction steel body/chassis structure. Four-seater, front engine/rear drive, sold as two-door closed coupé.

Engine
Type	Jaguar V12
Block material	Cast aluminium
Head material	Cast aluminium
Cylinders	12 in 60-degree vee
Cooling	Water
Bore and stroke	90 × 70mm
Capacity	5,343cc
Main bearings	7
Valves	2 per cylinder, operated by single-overhead camshaft per cylinder heads, and inverted bucket-type tappets
Compression ratio	9.0:1
Fuel supply	Bosch-Lucas fuel injection
Max. power	285bhp (DIN) @ 5,500rpm (USA: 244 @ 5,250rpm)
Max. torque	294lb.ft @ 3,500rpm (USA: 269 @ 4,500rpm)

Transmission
(Manual gearbox only available until 1979 – 352 such cars were produced)

Four-speed manual gearbox, with synchromesh on all forward gears

Clutch	Single dry plate, diaphragm spring; hydraulically operated

Internal gearbox ratios
Top	1.00:1
3rd	1.389:1
2nd	1.905:1
1st	3.238:1
Reverse	3.428:1
Final drive	3.07:1

Automatic transmission (Borg Warner) was optional from 1975–7.

Internal ratios
Direct	1.00:1
Intermediate	1.45:1
Low	2.40:1
Reverse	2.09:1
Max. torque multiplication	2.0:1
Final drive ratio	3.07:1

From April 1977: optional automatic transmission was by GM400.

Internal Ratios

Direct	1.00:1
Intermediate	1.48:1
Low	2.48:1
Reverse	2.09:1
Max. torque multiplication	2.0:1
Final drive ratio	3.07:1

Suspension and steering

Front	Independent, coil springs, wishbones, anti-roll bar, telescopic dampers
Rear	Independent, double coil springs, fixed-length drive shafts, lower wishbones, radius arms, twin telescopic dampers
Steering	Rack-and-pinion, power-assisted
Tyres	E70 205VR-15in, radial-ply
Wheels	Cast aluminium disc, bolt-on
Rim width	6.0in

Brakes

Type	Disc brakes at front and rear, with vacuum servo assistance
Size	11.8in diameter front, 10.4in diameter rear

Dimensions (in/mm)

Track	
Front	58/1,473
Rear	58.3/1,481
Wheelbase	102/2,591
Overall length	191.7/4,869
Overall width	70.6/1,793
Overall height	50.0/1,270
Unladen weight	3,859lb/1,750kg

NB. From mid-1980, the engine was re-rated with Lucas/Bosch digital electronic fuel injection, and a rise in compression ratio to 10.0:1. Peak figures were:

Max. power	300bhp (DIN) @ 5,400rpm (USA: 262bhp @ 5,000rpm)
Max. torque	318lb.ft @ 3,900rpm

seconds. Mind, you, 0–60mph took 25 seconds. Pointless? Yes, but quite remarkable...

The mass of text was full of praise for this complex car (the engine bay of which, by the way, was so full that the battery had to live in the boot, close to the fuel tank and the spare wheel) though there seemed to be reservations about the choice of ride/handling/suspension stiffness balance. *Autocar*, like most other testers at this time, often wondered about the rationale of 2+2 seating, commenting that:

In the back, the space is only occasional, except for children. A 6ft adult will request those in the front to move forward for the sake of his legs and head, which must be stooped to clear the roof.

73

Even so, the final summary told its own story:

Overall, the Jaguar XJ-S is superb. With very few exceptions, when you compare it with very nearly all of its competitors, it is not only still competitively priced, but a completely sorted motor car, giving the highest satisfaction. Jaguar really have done their development work, and one can appreciate why it took so long to appear. We envy those who can find a place for this most covetable motor car.

Motor was a little less enthusiastic about its own manual-transmission test car, and worried about the same dynamic qualities and the lack of space. On its cover it posed the question, 'Jaguar XJ-S: tank or super-car?' and in the opening summary the testers commented that it was:

A bit of both. It's larger, heavy, thirsty and cramped in the back. It's also superbly engineered, sensationally quick, very refined and magnificent to drive – a combination that no other car we've driven can match at the price.'

Along the way, *Motor* recorded very similar performance figures, but worse fuel consumption figures – 12.8mpg (22.1l/100km) was truly awful by any standards, especially as this was a period when the world's petrol prices seemed to be increasing steadily all the time.

Motor however, insisted on returning to the obvious conclusion that:

Despite what it is – an outrageously large and heavy 2-plus-2 seater – the Jaguar XJ-S is a magnificent motor car, not just for what it does but for the way it does it. The XJ-S combines a startling performance with exceptional smoothness and tractability and a standard of refinement that few cars can match.

In concept, the latest Jaguar must be regarded as a splendid anachronism... The only real criticism that could be levelled at the XJ-S is that it's dated in concept.

Finally, here is a look at what that arch-patriot (and Jaguar-lover) John Bolster had to say when he drove a manual-transmission XJ-S for an *Autosport* test in 1976. Headlining the piece 'Jaguar XJ-S: nothing but the best', he went on to describe it as a world-beater:

I shall not attempt to make any excuse for using a ton and three-quarters of extremely complicated machinery to carry me about for a week. If you tell me that I could have ridden a moped for six months on the same amount of petrol, you are going to get a very rude answer. I may be a bloated capitalist of the extreme right, but I loved every minute of it, so there!

A few wealthy Englishmen and a lot of rich foreigners will rush to buy the XJ-S, and it will make a great deal of money for British Leyland. As I have already said, a car of this price and performance is scarcely a logical buy, but as long as there is a demand for such exotica, Britain should endeavour to supply it. I've driven the German and Italian equivalents, and very nice they are too, but nobody who has tried them all could be in any possible doubt. The V12 from Coventry is the one, and if they can make them all as well as they built the car they lent me, Britain has a world-beater.

So far, so good, but the XJ-S still had to establish itself, particularly in North America – and this was where Jaguar was hoping to reap the majority of XJ-S orders. Mike Cook, who was running the North American Public Relations operation recalls that:

Jaguar's reputation for quality and reliability, at the time, was poor. MG and Triumph buyers didn't mind having to work on their cars, but Jaguar buyers were different. Doctors, dentists, lawyers and all kinds of professional people – they were used to being able to buy something and have it work, and if it didn't work they were used to being able to call up and have it fixed, right away.

The XJ-S buyer, after all, was paying premium money – a lot more than Cadillac money. [Cadillac prices started at $8,629 in 1976, whereas the XJ-S retailed at $19,000.]

But there was still an air of complacency from Browns Lane. Our people over here continually alerted the factory about problems, but they were not believed. The engineers did not believe, for instance, that our climate could get very hot – and stay hot.

The V12 engine, well, it had made a huge impact at first, because there hadn't been a volume-production V12 over here since the last Lincoln of 1948, so it was a real novelty. But, right away, there were problems, for the electronic ignition was set in the V, which was very neat and tidy – and completely in the wrong place – because this was the hottest part of the entire engine. So these things – the modules – would conk out. Right off the bat they were stopping on freeways, they were stopping in rush-hour traffic, they were dying all over the country.

Although Jaguar eventually cured such problems, this was an example of the baggage that the XJ-S had to carry when it went on sale. There was still the question of image, too:

It was difficult to give the XJ-S a reputation at first, because of its appearance, and the departure from what had been sold before – for it was a successor to, rather than a replacement for, the E-Type.

The auto writers, whether enthusiast or business press, wandered around it and scratched their heads, because they really didn't know what it was supposed to be. It became instantly obvious that it wasn't a sports car – it handled well, it went well, it was very comfortable, nice and quiet, all of which made it just like other Jaguars.

It was a puzzle. The dealers had a difficult job selling it at first.

Graham Whitehead, who was running the North American operation, confirms this impression:

The people who were going to buy the XJ-S were different from those who had bought E-Types. In fact the XJ-S was very difficult to sell in the first few years – early sales were disappointing, so much so that it was not a significant part of our programme.

It was because of the difficulty in establishing an image – one which, after all, was so very different from that of the well-loved E-Type – that the XJ-S made such a slow start in North America. As in the UK, testers loved the straight line performance, the ride and the handling, but most of them were appalled by the heavy fuel consumption – and there were often obvious quality problems.

A *Road Test* writer struggled with their thoughts, eventually admitting that:

It's more than a little eerie. It never ruffled its feathers, never tried to turn round and snap. It just flexed its broad shoulders and worked.

This was *exactly* what Jaguar wanted everyone to think – on the other hand they did not want *Car & Driver* to conclude that the facia design was 'pure [Ford] Pinto', or that it was:

(Left) *When the XJ-S was being built at Browns Lane, the V12 engine/transmission unit had to be slotted in from above. ...*

... though the body shell was first dropped on to the already-assembled front and rear suspension units.

... a dark and mysterious product of England's tortured auto-industry, fantastically over-qualified for today's driving conditions.

Even so, British Leyland would have to live with the car as it stood, for several years at least, as finances were so strapped in this period that very little money could be spent on improving the XJ-S in the late 1970s. Apart from essential work to meet North American legislation, and to improve the car's reliability, there were no visual changes for five years.

The only significant mechanical improvements in this period were that the modern GM Type 400 automatic transmission took over from the old style Borg Warner Model 12 transmission in April 1977, and that a revised, fully digital, Bosch-Lucas electronic fuel injection system was introduced in mid-1980. In that period, also, two minor style 'packages' were introduced – one early in February 1978, the other in April 1979.

By the end of 1977, British Leyland were in a mess, with the so-called 'Ryder Plan' discredited, with strikes proliferating all over the ramshackle empire, and with horrendous losses mounting. It was no wonder that the XJ-S had to soldier on without major change – for Jaguar's product action at this time was concentrated on the XJ6/XJ12 saloons, which became Series III in the spring of 1979.

CORPORATE UPHEAVAL

Following the abrupt resignation of British Leyland chairman Sir Richard Dobson in October 1977, the pugnacious South African-born Michael Edwardes took his place as chairman and chief executive.

Within days it was clear that Edwardes not only intended to shake up the empire, but had been given a free hand to impose whatever changes he proposed. During the winter, to Jaguar's delight, he dismantled the unwieldy 'Leyland Cars' operation and re-established Jaguar as an operating company – though it was still only one of three major businesses in Jaguar-Rover-Triumph.

The good news was that the Radford machining and sub-assembly plant (old hands in Coventry still referred to this factory as 'The Daimler') now came back under Jaguar Cars' direct control. At the same time, there was more direct access, and influence, to Castle Bromwich, where the XJ-S body shell was built.

Although this was almost precisely the structure proposed by Geoffrey Robinson in 1974, Jaguar still did not have total freedom. From 1978, however, they once again gained some operating autonomy, and a new managing director – Bob Knight.

Knight's appointment was a surprise to almost everyone, whether inside Jaguar or out, for this quiet, studious, deep-thinking engineer, a chain-smoking, life-long bachelor, was not the forceful sort of character the business seemed to need. No one certainly could see Bob as the sort of pugnacious, hard-talking boss that Jaguar surely needed at that time of industrial anarchy and constant dispute.

Michael Edwardes, however, certainly seemed to be impressed – especially after Knight had sailed through the compulsory written psychological tests that Edwardes imposed on all his top management team in 1977/1978. As Knight's one-time boss, Geoffrey Robinson, reminded me:

Bob was a terrific guy, but a notoriously slow decision maker, and very reclusive – however, he'd obviously studied the requirements of this 'shrink test' before he took it, and came out of it as a quick decision maker, and on the personal side as a very caring husband! He came to see me afterwards, and told me how he was very pleased to have beaten the system.

Although Bob Knight was exactly the right man Jaguar needed to head up its engineering team – all the work on the 1980s XJ-S HE models, and on the new-generation six-cylinder engines was started up under his control – almost no one except Michael Edwardes could visualize him as the managing director Jaguar needed at this time. Mike Cook recalls the problem:

Bob was very quiet, studious, scholarly – but spoke very softly, and without force. When Bob came over to the USA, the dealers didn't really know what to make of him. He would sit there, holding up his cigarette in that unique manner, smiling amiably through the smoke...

OK, maybe he was the guy who kept the company in existence for two years, but it was John Egan who brought it back to life.

At the end of the 1970s, in fact, Jaguar's quality image had sunk to an all-time low, the new XJ6/XJ12 Series III cars developed had a richly earned appalling reliability reputation at first, which dragged the XJ-S down with them – and the V12 engine had been hit by the second Energy Crisis/Oil Shock.

XJ-S production, which had peaked early, at 3,890 cars in 1977, then halved within two years. The problem, according to BL chairman Michael Edwardes was not in its engineering, but in the running of the Jaguar business:

It was obvious that Jaguar was losing a great deal of money – losses were running at millions of pounds a year. The attitude problem was enormous; the men on the shop floor, and indeed many of the managers, still considered Jaguar to be elite, and their own contribution to be unique. Some managers [This must refer to Bob Knight, surely?] were more concerned with producing new models and reaching new standards of engineering excellence than with managing the business.

It proved difficult to get across to them the simple fact that Jaguar was not being managed ...

At this point, make no mistake, the XJ-S project was virtually dead in the water, and for a time there was a real danger that it would soon be cancelled completely. With money-men, rather than a patriarch like Sir William Lyons, now controlling Jaguar's fortunes, sentiment and personal pride were not factors. Not only that, but we now know that BL bosses even considered closing down Jaguar completely, for in 1979 a mere 14,861 cars had been built at Browns Lane, of which a miserable 3,185 were sent to the USA. The XJ-S suffered as badly, if not worse, than any other Jaguar model. At this point it was still a marketing failure and prospects were not good. Between 1975 and 1979 only 13,743 XJ-S cars had been built and, worse, a mere 4,266 of them had been sold in the USA.

Irritated, no doubt, by his mistake in appointing Bob Knight to the 'Mission Impossible' task, Edwardes sacked him (there was no phasing out, or hand-over, period) – and sent in a tough, hard-talking, manager called John Egan.

Egan (like Geoffrey Robinson before him) arrived at Browns Lane on a day when the production lines were at a standstill, but his brief was clear – he had to make Jaguar work, or close it down!

For the XJ-S, as for everyone at Jaguar, the next few months would be critical.

5 The HE Generation – and JaguarSport

Although John Egan arrived at Jaguar in April 1980 when the company was at a low ebb, it was not all bad news for Jaguar followers. And even though the latest Series III XJ6/XJ12 types were being built badly, they had received a friendly reception from dealers, customers and the media. Development and engineering work on the XJ-S was still going ahead, and although the current car was selling slowly, there was great hope for the future.

If the XJ-S was to be rescued from certain oblivion, everyone at Jaguar knew what had to be done – it would need to be freshened up, made more economical, and somehow it would also need a speedy injection of more 'Jaguarness', particularly regarding its style and its furnishing.

Jaguar knew this, and reacted swiftly in the short term; in the medium term there were also plans to provide an open-top alternative, and a new range of six-cylinder engines. None of that, however, could possibly be achieved until money could be found for capital investment – and that would have to wait.

Although Michael Edwardes' brief to John Egan – Mission Impossible, some thought at the time – was to turn round the entire operation, and bring it back to greatness, this was never going to be easy. As Edwardes himself has written:

> Bridges were built with the workforce from that first day. John Egan believed what

other Jaguar executives would not: that Jaguar's mounting losses made Jaguar's demise a certainty unless the turn-round could be accomplished so quickly that the 1981 Plan would show a vast improvement and the company could project a break-even, or better still a profit, for 1982. There was no other way in which major investment in the new light-weight engine could be justified ...

Egan set a new agenda from the moment that he arrived at Browns Lane, not only in convincing the sometimes bloody-minded workforce that the British taxpayer did not owe them a living, but, equally important, in convincing scores of suppliers that the quality of their components would have to improve drastically if the company was to survive. As Egan once quipped, in an aside:

> I actually managed to convince wheel suppliers that their wheels should be round ...

History records that the Jaguar company was effectively reborn in the early 1980s, as this very simple table proves:

Year	Jaguar Production	Jaguar XJ-S Production
1979	14,861	2,405
1980	15,262	1,057
1981	13,812	1,292
1982	21,934	3,478
1983	27,331	4,749

Note, however, that it was getting on for two years before the Egan revolution began to pay off. Production and sales were no better in 1981 than they had been in 1980 – but then the recovery was dramatic. By 1983 production of Jaguars had doubled, with XJ-S production already up by more than 400 per cent, and due to soar yet further.

This, and a similar recovery by the XJ6 and XJ12 saloons, meant that Jaguar rapidly moved from making horrendous losses to making healthy profits. In 1980, the year in which John Egan took over, Jaguar had lost £47.3 million on a turnover of £166.4 million, but by 1983 (when the move to privatization began) the company was making profits of £50 million on a turnover of £476 million.

HE – A TECHNICAL LEAP FORWARD

The XJ-S's rebirth dates from July 1981 and the launch of the much-revised HE model. It was not before time, for XJ-S sales had been so slow in 1979–80 that the car had actually been taken out of production for some months to allow stocks (particularly in the USA) to be run down.

The HE (which stood for 'High Efficiency') package was worked up in the late 1970s, and although most attention centred around changes to the V12 engine, significant improvements were also made to the car's style and equipment, both externally and inside the cabin. However, because of

Visually there were many detail differences between the V12 HE engine (this example) and the earlier fuel-injected types, mostly connected with the layout of fuel rails. There was also a general tidying up of the under-bonnet layout.

the low sales so far achieved, a restyle, or even a major facelift, could not be justified.

This meant, in effect, that there was no 1980–81 model as such, for it took management a great deal of time to make the significant jump from the digital-electronic-ignition 1980 model to what the Americans always call the '82 Model Year HE.

Changes to the engine were inspired by independent research work pioneered by a Swiss engineer (and one-time racing driver) Michael May. By the mid-1970s he had come to concentrate on ways of improving an engine's combustion efficiency – by releasing more power, more fuel efficiency, or both – and soon let Europe's industry know what he was doing.

Jaguar's top engine man Harry Mundy, a hands-on and ruthlessly practical engineer with decades of experience in his craft, would normally have been cynical about such claims of 'power-for-free' – he had, after all, spent years at BRM where such notions were delivered with the morning milk – but was soon convinced when May's theories were backed up in testing at Browns Lane.

Michael May's principle was that the compression ratio could be raised considerably, but that there should be much more 'swirl' of the fuel/air flow as it passed through the ports and past the valves: along with changes to the combustion chamber layout, this was given the exciting name of the 'Fireball' head.

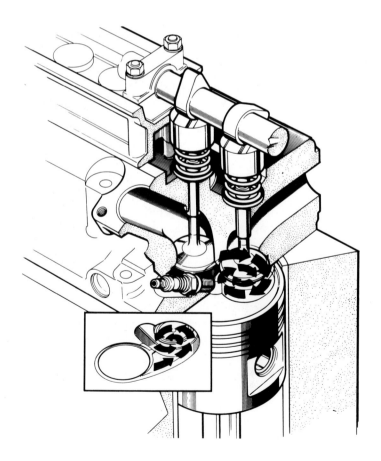

Michael May's 'Fireball' theories and techniques were adopted for the XJ-S HE of 1981. Not only was there much more swirl as fuel/air mixture entered the cylinders, but the combustion chamber was now located in the crown of the piston, close to the exhaust valve. The basic single-cam layout, though, was not changed.

The basic change to the V12 engine's cylinder head, though sounding simple, was aerodynamically complex. In the original Jaguar V12, the combustion chamber was formed in the top of the piston (the classic 'bowl-in-piston' layout, first seen in the UK in the Rover 2000), the cylinder head face being absolutely flat. In the 'Fireball head', this layout was reversed, with the piston crown being absolutely flat, and with a small combustion chamber, featuring very complex curvatures and profiles, being formed in a new cylinder head casting, and concentrated around the exhaust valve: the compression ratio was no less than 12.5:1.

This, together with leaner fuel injection settings, seemed to make all the difference. In theory, a leaner mixture, allied to the higher compression ratio, should mean that the combustion was more complete and thus more efficient – and so it was.

Jaguar announced that they had spent £500,000 on providing new cylinder head castings, making changes to the plant at Radford, and providing for other related changes, which, incidentally, were not immediately adopted for the XJ12 saloon. Even then, this looked like small change – if it paid off in practice.

The proof, incidentally, came very soon. According to independent road tests, UK-spec. XJ-S cars could now record 16.3mpg (17.4l/100km) instead of 14mpg (20l/100km), while less powerful USA-spec. cars could record 14.9mpg (US gallons) instead of 13mpg (19l/100km instead of 22). In both cases, that represented around 15 per cent better fuel efficiency – which in those days of rapidly escalating fuel prices was well worth having. As Mike Cook told me:

When the first Fuel Crisis came along in 1973, I was buying gasoline in the USA for 35 cents/gallon, but by the time the XJ-S came along it was up to $1/gallon. Then, we

were looking at prices eventually going up to the sort of level they are now in Europe. That never happened, but it always bothered people.

Now, in the early 1980s, we were into the 'Gas Guzzler' period. It was a fight between Jaguar, Rolls-Royce and Ferrari as to who could get the worst gas mileage, and in its original form the XJ-S got about 9mpg (US) – 9mpg, can you believe this? That was idiotic, even with fuel injection, it could only get 9mpg!

Then the HE came out, and right away it was doing up to 14mpg, which was a lot better. Suddenly, Jaguar was contributing to saving the environment, so we tried to make a lot of that …

I honestly believe that the rebirth of the XJ-S started from then. People's perception of the car was entirely different – it was a much better car. It wasn't great, but it was a hell of a lot better.

The sales graph turned up right away, but the XJ-S couldn't have accomplished this on its own – it was being pulled along by the other cars. This was the 'John Egan factor', the rebirth of Jaguar in the USA.

With such an improvement, of course, all thought of bringing in an XK-engined version of the XJ-S could be abandoned (this option was considered, though little work was ever done), and the lack of a smaller, six-cylinder engine was no longer quite as serious a problem.

The engine change, of course, was just one factor in the HE package. To match the increased power, torque and fuel-efficiency, the rear axle ratio was raised to 2.88:1 (but since one could hardly hear the engine in motion, the average owner rarely noticed), and of course all cars were now fitted with the latest GM400 automatic transmission.

A few, but important, suspension changes were brought in at the same time – notably

For the HE derivative, Jaguar adopted new-style 'Starfish' five-spoke alloy wheels, along with other detailing like smoother bumpers and the pin-stripes along the flanks.

the fitment of 215/70-15 tyres on new-style 6.5in rim alloy wheels, in place of the original 205/70-15 tyres with 6.0in rim wheel combination. In almost every way the new wheels looked simpler, more sporty and altogether more 'butch' than the earlier variety.

Detail changes to the exterior style included the use of rubber-faced bumpers which extended around the flanks, larger pin stripes along the sides of the car, and integral rear fog guard lamps built into the rear bumpers.

The major appearance change, however, came inside the car, where the latest XJ-S was finally given the 'traditional' Jaguar wood veneer that had so conspicuously been

absent from 1975 to 1981. At a stroke, it seemed, Jaguar had returned the XJ-S to its roots. The upgraded interior included all-leather trim, elm veneer infills on the dash and door cappings (burr walnut would not be used until the mid-1980s) a revised steering wheel (rather like that of the latest XJ6 SIII saloon), and revised switchgear. 'Unseens' included key-operated central locking, delay-wiper wipers, electrically adjustable door mirrors and much more.

The entire package was signalled, not only by different badging, but by the inclusion of 'HE' lettering on the boot lid.

For Jaguar traditionalists, the major surprise was that Michael May's work was

The XJ-S HE of 1981 was the first of this type to feature a wooden dashboard – elm veneer being chosen for this period – the impression being much more that of a traditional Jaguar than ever before.

Michael May (born 1936)

In 1981 he seemed to come from nowhere and, as far as Jaguar followers were concerned, he soon faded back into obscurity. Although widely credited with the 'Fireball' cylinder head changes made to inspire the HE version of the Jaguar V12 engine, Michael May was not involved (publicly, at least) in any other Jaguar work.

Born in Switzerland in 1936, May trained as an engineer but still found time to involve himself in motor racing along the way. Even then, he was an inventor, for in 1956 he had tested a large transverse rear spoiler on a Porsche 550 two-seater racing sports car – although this car was not allowed to race as officials thought the spoiler might be dangerous.

After becoming European Formula Junior Champion, he concentrated solely on business. As an independent consulting engineer, starting in 1970, he developed theories about stratified charge engines, finding ways of reshaping combustion spaces to be much more fuel-efficient – with higher compression ratios, and using much leaner-than-normal air/fuel ratios.

Working from Rolle, on the lakeside between Geneva and Lausanne, May's company, Antipollution Industrial Research SA, developed its theories in VW Passat engines, publishing its conclusions in 1976. A Jaguar development contract soon followed, and the 'HE' engine was the result.

actually mentioned – saluted, even – by the company when the XJ-S HE was launched. It would never have happened, some said, in Sir William's time – for although Sir William had also used many consultants, there had sometimes been a reluctance to admit this to the world at large.

Not only was the HE an altogether better and more appealing package than the original-style XJ-S which it replaced, but it was brought in at a sharply reduced price. In Britain and in North America prices were still rising unstoppably, but this did not deter Jaguar from taking a major gamble.

When it was launched in July 1981 (deliveries in the USA started within weeks), the new-type XJ-S HE was listed at £18,950,

which compared with £19,763 for the last of the pre-HE models. Although this was only a reduction of 4.1 per cent, it was also a very real £813 – or, putting this in 1981 motor car terms, this was a quarter of the way to buying a Mini as a runabout.

Following the appearance of the HE, sales – and the XJ-S's reputation – turned up almost at once. Browns Lane passed its low point, all the indicators pointed upwards instead of downwards, Jaguar people started smiling again instead of pursing their lips, and all thought of abandoning the project were forgotten.

Graham Whitehead recalls that it was the entire Jaguar range, not merely the XJ-S, which was reborn at this point. 'The Egan

From the rear, Jaguar made the arrival of the HE quite obvious – by adding the 'HE' badges to the tail panel. There were no changes to the sheet metal.

Jaguar XJ-S HE 5.3-Litre (1981–91)

Layout

Unit-construction steel body/chassis structure. Four-seater, front engine/rear drive, sold as two-door closed coupé throughout, Cabriolet from 1985–88, Convertible from 1988–91.

Engine

Type	Jaguar V12
Block material	Cast aluminium
Head material	Cast aluminium
Cylinders	12 in 60-degree vee
Cooling	Water
Bore and stroke	90 × 70mm
Capacity	5,343cc
Main bearings	7
Valves	2 per cylinder, operated by single-overhead camshaft per cylinder heads, and inverted bucket-type tappets
Compression ratio	12.5:1
Fuel supply	Bosch-Lucas fuel injection

1981–88

Max. power	299bhp (DIN) @ 5,500rpm (USA: 262bhp @ 5,000rpm)
Max. torque	318lb.ft @ 3,500rpm (USA: 290lb.ft @ 3,000rpm)

1988–91

Max. power	291bhp (DIN) @ 5,500rpm (USA: 262bhp @ 5,000rpm)
Max. torque	317lb.ft @ 3,000rpm (USA: 290lb.ft @ 3,000rpm)

Transmission

Manual gearbox not available. Automatic transmission (GM400 type) standard.

Internal ratios

Direct	1.00:1
Intermediate	1.48:1
Low	2.48:1
Reverse	2.09:1
Maximum torque multiplication	2.0:1
Final drive ratio	2.88:1

Suspension and steering

Front	Independent, coil springs, wishbones, anti-roll bar, telescopic dampers
Rear	Independent, double coil springs, fixed length drive shafts, lower wishbones, radius arms, twin telescopic dampers
Steering	Rack-and-pinion, power-assisted
Tyres	(To 1988): 215/70VR-15in, radial-ply; (from 1988): 235/60VR-15in
Wheels	Cast aluminium disc, bolt-on
Rim width	6.5in

Brakes	
Type	Disc brakes at front and rear, with vacuum servo assistance
Size	11.8in diameter front, 10.40in diameter rear

Dimensions (in/mm)	
Track	
Front	58/1,473
Rear	58.3/1,481
Wheelbase	102/2,591
Overall length	191.7/4,869
Overall width	70.6/1,793
Overall height	50.0/1,270
Unladen weight	Coupé 3,859lb/1,750kg
	Cabriolet 3,920lb/1,778kg
	Convertible 4,055lb/1,835kg

Effect' became evident all over the world, as sales rushed up. Within four years overall production at Browns Lane had more than doubled, without any major change in models or in assembly facilities:

> The dealer organization was selling more and more of the sedan, so the XJ-S rode on the back of that success. After a certain length of time the bandwagon effect took over.

NEW MODELS

This, though, was only the start. All over the developed world, it seemed, there was an economic boom. Countries were getting more prosperous, new millionaires were created and the demand for Jaguars soared. Although the arrival of the six-cylinder engined XJ-SC (see Chapter 6) did not make a huge difference to the numbers, it widened the range considerably – all adding to the impression that Jaguar were serious about expanding their range, serious about modernization, and serious about producing all types of cars for all their customers.

Looking back, it was the launch of the SC model that signalled Jaguar's determination to make a long-term success of this range. In the first eight years of its career, there had only been one major modification – the arrival of the HE in mid-1981 – but thereafter there seemed to be important innovation almost every year. To those who were still critical of the car's looks, Jaguar could point at the rising sales figures – and continue to make a car looking the same way that it always had.

Yet another new model arrived in July 1985, this being the V12-engined version of the SC Cabriolet – Jaguar, like Ford and GM it seemed, had little to learn about the mix-and-match process. The new derivative, only available with automatic transmission, carried the unwieldy title of XJ-S HE V12 Cabriolet, and brought the possibility of 150mph (240km/h) open-air motoring back to Jaguar for the first time in a decade.

As with the smaller-engined variety, this was a pure two-seater, with a platform and stowage lockers in the redundant 'rear seat' area. Not only was it a colossally rapid machine, but, as with all other XJ-S types, it was fitted with air conditioning as

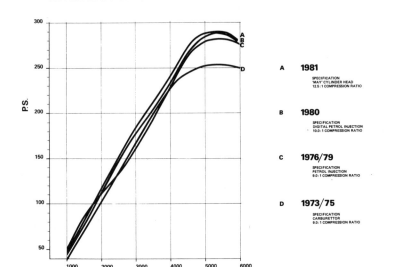

V12 Engine Performance BHP Comparison
EUROPEAN SPECIFICATION DIN TEST

A **1981**
SPECIFICATION
'MAY' CYLINDER HEAD
12.5:1 COMPRESSION RATIO

B **1980**
SPECIFICATION
DIGITAL PETROL INJECTION
10.0:1 COMPRESSION RATIO

C **1976/79**
SPECIFICATION
PETROL INJECTION
9.0:1 COMPRESSION RATIO

D **1973/75**
SPECIFICATION
CARBURETTOR
9.0:1 COMPRESSION RATIO

When the HE was launched, Jaguar issued these two very significant graphs, showing how the power and torque of the V12 engine had improved so much since it had been launched. Curves identified 'C' refer to the original XJ-S, those marked 'B' to the 1980/81 digital injection engines, and those marked 'A' to the new 'Fireball' engine. It is obvious from the torque curves that the latest digital injection had already worked wonders for the V12's breathing, even before the HE Installation arrived.

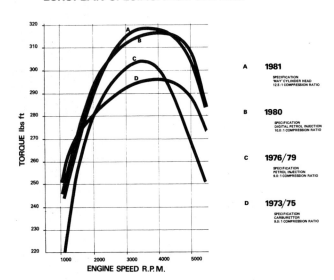

V12 Engine Performance Torque Comparison
EUROPEAN SPECIFICATION DIN TEST

A **1981**
SPECIFICATION
'MAY' CYLINDER HEAD
12.5:1 COMPRESSION RATIO

B **1980**
SPECIFICATION
DIGITAL PETROL INJECTION
10.0:1 COMPRESSION RATIO

C **1976/79**
SPECIFICATION
PETROL INJECTION
9.0:1 COMPRESSION RATIO

D **1973/75**
SPECIFICATION
CARBURETTOR
9.0:1 COMPRESSION RATIO

(Opposite)
Two views of the XJ-SC V12 Cabriolet, which was introduced in 1975. This combined the cabriolet style first seen with the new AJ6 six-cylinder engine, and the existing V12 engine and running gear.

standard. The fact that driving a drop-top XJ-S at high speeds was rather a noisy and blustery business did not matter to open-air enthusiasts. In California, after all, one could cruise at whatever speed the Highway Patrol would ignore, yet still sit comfortably on leather seats in the cool of an air-conditioned cockpit. This, at least, was half-way towards the sort of car that the North American dealer chain had been requesting for some years.

In the UK the mid-1985 price line-up of the four-model range was:

XJ-SC 3.6 Coupé	£20,395
XJ-SC 3.6 Cabriolet	£22,395
XJ-S HE Coupé	£24,995
XJ-SC HE V12 Cabriolet	£26,995

Two mid-1980s XJ-S V12 models – the Cabriolet and the Coupé, posed in a group with the existing Jaguar (and Daimler) saloons in 1985, in the driveway of Sir William Lyons's house at Wappenbury Hall in Warwickshire.

PRIVATIZATION

World-wide, as the XJ-S range expanded, overall sales rose inexorably. From the low point of 1,057 cars in 1980, and the great recovery to 4,749 in 1983, production kept on increasing, reaching 7,951 in 1985, and 9,052 in 1986. Some of this, in fact, was due to the favourable publicity caused by the privatization of Jaguar, which made headlines all around the world. Privatization freed Jaguar from government finance and control, and was thus an event of cataclysmic importance for the marque, finally restoring the independence that Jaguar had lost in 1966 when Sir William Lyons agreed to join forces with BMC. After eighteen turbulent years, Jaguar were back where they had always deserved to be – on their own, in the spotlight, making all their own decisions.

With the Conservatives coming to power in 1979, the government's attitude to state-owned businesses had changed completely. Prime Minister Margaret Thatcher made it clear that she wanted to pull the state out of as many enterprises as possible – especially those that were losing money! Entrepreneurs, she reasoned, would always be willing to take on the loss-makers, for such people had the confidence to attempt a turnround the government could never achieve.

Because it was apparently not yet practical to sell off the BL combine as a complete business (although this was considered, no suitable buyer, or offer, was ever found), the government decided to separate Jaguar from the balance of the operation (which meant that Austin-Morris and the Leyland Truck & Bus sectors would continue to be state-owned) and float it as the 'jewel in the crown'. In December 1983 the government revealed that it intended to sell Jaguar and Unipart (the spares business) as going concerns during 1984, when there was huge interest from the financial community.

The 'float' was formalized in May 1984, when a new company, Jaguar plc, was set up. John Egan, naturally, would be chief executive, while Hamish Orr-Ewing would be the non-executive chairman in the first year. Graham Whitehead of Jaguar Cars Inc. (the trading subsidiary in the USA) also joined the board, as did Ray Horrocks (as a non-executive), who would remain as a top director in the remainder of BL Ltd.

The 'float' took place early in August when the government arranged for 177,880,000 ordinary shares (nominally rated at 25 pence each) to go on sale at 165 pence/share, which instantly raised nearly £300 million for HM Treasury. Because of Jaguar's booming reputation, demand far exceeded supply, and the value of the shares on the stock market surged ahead (and would continue to rise until the take-over by Ford in 1989). At the time, incidentally, few bothered to read the 'small print', in which the government retained what was nicknamed a 'Golden Share', and ultimate control; this effectively meant that Jaguar plc could not then be taken over by another company or investor without the agreement of the government.

When Jaguar plc reported on their first year of trading (for 1984), the two figures that mattered were the turnover of more than £600 million, and profits of no less than £91.5 million. This, by a very long way, was the most money that Jaguar had ever made in a year.

For the next few years the XJ-S's fortunes developed on two fronts – V12-engined and six-cylinder engined types – so for clarity I have decided to discuss the AJ6-engined six-cylinder types in the next chapter. For the next few years, in any case, the specification of the V12-engined car altered only slowly.

Burr walnut wood cappings finally replaced burr elm in the autumn of 1985, then at the beginning of 1987 there was a

Even by the late 1980s, the V12-engined cars were visually little changed from the originals, though experts will now note the use of different road wheels and yet another version of the badging.

facia/interior facelift featuring a new central switchgear layout and a more smoothly profiled centre console, along with a new steering wheel style.

From 1985 to 1987 Jaguar managers had to leave the XJ-S to its own devices for a time, as they were not only tied up with the proving and launch of the new-generation XJ6 saloon (known by one and all, before its launch, as the 'XJ40', which was its project code), but with the development of the new design/development centre at Whitley.

Although Rootes, and later Chrysler United Kingdom Ltd, had already spent a great deal of money on the development of this ex-Armstrong-Whitworth aerospace plant, Jaguar spent a whole lot more

(Opposite, above) The Whitley technical centre, south-east of Coventry's city centre, looks big enough to assemble cars in series – but is purely used by Jaguar for styling, engineering and proving purposes. This shot was taken while reconstruction work was still going ahead. The styling department is to centre-right, and features an outside viewing area with a high wall to frustrate prying eyes!

(Opposite, below) By 1988 Jaguar had completed the transformation of the ex-Rootes, ex-Chrysler, ex-Peugeot technical centre at Whitley, Coventry, and taken it over as a design, engineering and development headquarters. Current models, at the time, were the XJ-S and the new-generation 'XJ40' XJ6 saloon.

between 1985 and 1988. Critics of the flamboyant John Egan insist, to this day, that money spent at Whitley should have gone into improving the production cars instead. There were those who suggested that Karmann's services would not have been needed on the convertible if so much money had not been spent at Whitley.

In some ways, however, the capital lavished on facilities at Whitley helped the development of the XJ-S considerably. Not only was there much space for engine test and development workshops, but entire buildings were devoted to exhaust emissions work and endurance driving vehicles. In addition, for the first time during the

company's long history, Jaguar would have a modern and sizeable styling facility with extensive indoor and outdoor viewing facilities – all a great advance on the 'make-do' layout at Browns Lane.

Even so, the fact remains that the glossy face of Whitley was very different from the old fashioned conditions that persisted inside some of Browns Lane's factory blocks. Yet, in a way, one can only congratulate John Egan for painting a bright smile on Jaguar while saving money on what could not be seen from outside. It was not until after they had taken control of Jaguar that Ford discovered how much they would have to spend on upgrading the assembly lines.

By the mid-1980s XJ-S assembly was carried out on some of the same tracks as those of the saloons.

Thus it was that the full convertible did not finally arrive until the spring of 1988 – nearly thirteen years after the original XJ-S had been launched – an event which has to be described in the next chapter.

JAGUARSPORT

Tom Walkinshaw's successful motor racing campaign on behalf of Jaguar is detailed in Chapter 9, and it is now a matter of record that he eventually expanded those links to set up JaguarSport, and to build the XJ220 'Supercar'. Looking back, though, it seems to have taken a long time for Walkinshaw's image-improving racing programme to spill over to production cars.

Walkinshaw's original aim was 'to produce limited volumes of uniquely styled, high-performance cars, which will help broaden the marque's appeal to customers who require their Jaguars to have more overt sporting characteristics'. At first JaguarSport set out to produce up to 500 cars a year, though in the end sales never rose far enough to approach that limit. By the early 1990s the line had closed down.

Tom Walkinshaw (born 1946)

Although his first connection with Jaguar came in 1981/2, Tom Walkinshaw had already succeeded in two careers by that time – first as a racing driver, then as a businessman.

Born in Prestonpans, near Edinburgh, he started racing in 1966, using an MG Midget, progressing to single-seater Formula Ford cars in 1968, and to F3 by 1970. He then turned successfully to touring cars, racing Fords and BMWs with great success, and then set up TWR (Tom Walkinshaw Racing) in 1976.

By 1981 TWR had expanded considerably, not only preparing and selling racing saloons, but selling engine tune-up and body dress-up kits for manufacturers such as BMW GB and Mazda UK. From 1982 he first started racing Jaguars – the Group A XJ-S machines of 1982–87 – his links with Jaguar becoming stronger and closer with every year which passed.

To follow the XJ-S programme TWR began racing specially built mid-engined racing sports cars, starting with the XJR-5s in 1985 and culminating with the XJR-14s in 1991. Along the way the cars won twice at Le Mans – in 1988 and 1990 – won the World Sports Car Championship, and also developed a new Metro 6R4-based turbocharged V6 engine for the early 1990s. There was also a successful North American IMSA programme.

Walkinshaw and his companies seemed to possess boundless energy, for at this time he also set up a new joint company – JaguarSport Ltd – with Jaguar to manufacture special versions of Jaguar road cars, became chairman of the Silverstone group for a controversial four years, and presided over the development and production of the mid-engined Jaguar XJ220 'Supercar' project, in which 271 cars were made.

But there was more. In the early 1990s he not only sold half of his business to Benetton, but became a major force in that Formula 1 team, later adding control of the Ligier F1 team to his interests. And there was even more. Once Ford financed Aston Martin's new DB7 project, they made sure that Walkinshaw and his factories were closely involved. Then, from 1994, TWR began running the official Volvo British Touring Car effort, and there were strong signs that even closer links with the Swedish company would follow.

By the mid-1990s TWR had interests in several continents, in production cars and racing cars, having taken control of the Arrows F1 team in 1996. It was no wonder that Walkinshaw himself needed a helicopter to flit from appointment to appointment. Was there no end to his ambitions?

Before Jaguar approved the Walkinshaw scheme, they had already been approached by several other concerns, but until TWR made their presentation, none had offered the credibility which made the proposition attractive.

JaguarSport Ltd – a company owned 50 per cent by Jaguar and 50 per cent by TWR – was officially launched in May 1988, its first product being a special version of the XJ-S, to be known as the XJR-S. Assembly of road cars was to be based at Kidlington, north of Oxford, close to the famous workshop that prepared and raced the famous racing sports cars. Initially twenty-two

selected Jaguar dealers became JaguarSport agents – though as the years progressed the net was widened further.

Bill Donnelly, then sales and marketing manager of JaguarSport, told me:

> One of JaguarSport's main objectives, the reason it was set up, was to begin changing the reputation and character of the cars. During the 1970s and 1980s the character of the production cars had changed. Most people accept that they gradually became more luxurious and more comfortable, but that they lost that sporting edge.

V12 engine for motor racing

Jaguar's famous V12 engine was originally conceived in the 1950s as a twin-overhead-camshaft (per bank) racing unit. The first engine, completed in 1964, was actually a racing 5-litre that produced 502bhp, but it was not further developed in that form. The single-cam (per bank) V12 that went into production was a very different design in many ways.

The first racing application of the single-cam V12 was developed by Broadspeed in 1976 and 1977: this was a 'Group 2' unit for the XJ12 four-seater 'Coupé' and produced about 500bhp. This racing programme was short-lived, but in the USA Bob Tullius' Group 44 team, with factory backing, produced successful 476bhp versions to win the Trans-Am Championship.

Tom Walkinshaw then started again with the Group A XJ-S cars in 1982, and by 1984 these TWR engines were producing a reliable 450bhp. Then, as later, many of the TWR pieces were manufactured by Cosworth Engineering, though most of the actual development of the cars was done by TWR at Kidlington, north of Oxford.

Then came the two interrelated Group C and IMSA racing sports car programmes of the late 1980s, in which TWR (Group C) and Bob Tullius' Group 44 (IMSA) teams were involved. The TWR achievements give an idea of what was achieved at this time.

The 1985 XJR-5's engine was a 6.2-litre/650bhp unit, the 1986 XJR-6 used a 6.5-litre/700bhp unit while for 1987 the XJR-8 used a 7-litre engine with a similar power output. All these engines used modified versions of the original 'flat-head' single-cam cylinder heads. By this stage, too, TWR had also taken over the North American IMSA programme, where engines were limited to 6 litres.

By the late 1980s TWR had also developed their own 4-valves-per-cylinder twin-cam cylinder head for the racing engine, and found that there was still scope for the engine to be further enlarged. For the 1991 Le Mans 24-Hour race, however, the well-proven XJR-12 race car was equipped with single-cam engines, but these had been enlarged to 7.4 litres and developed 730bhp at 7,000rpm. The torque of that engine was an astonishing 610lb.ft at 5,500rpm.

The measure of TWR's abilities was that in seven years the basic production V12 had been transformed, having been enlarged from 5.3 litres to 7.4 litres, and had seen its 300bhp road-car power figure increased by nearly 250 per cent.

(Left) *Jaguar's famous badge/trade-mark –*
known affectionately as the 'Grinner' by
Jaguar enthusiasts.

(Above) *It all depends what*
you are looking for in a car –
the late-1980s style of an XJ-S
Coupé, or the early 1950s
shape of an XK120 Coupé. 2+2
or two-seater, V12 or six-
cylinder? Make up your own
mind …

The XJ-S facia, as re-styled
without 'drum' style auxiliary
instruments for the major
facelift of 1991.

(Above) *From the side, the HE was immediately recognizable by the new-style five-spoke alloy wheels.*

(Left) *The final XJS instrument / facia panel of the 1990s was beautifully, and comprehensively, detailed.*

Although the re-styled car incorporated different rear quarter window shapes, there was no more exposed glass than before, as a careful study of this shot confirms.

(Left) Working on the XJ-S's V12 engine was not for the faint-hearted! This layout was gradually tidied up as the years passed – but the bonnet was always completely full.

(Right) From the rear, the only way to 'pick' an HE from its predecessor was by the badging and the new-style bumper/fog guard lamps.

For every market in the world except the USA, one aspect of the XJ-S/XJS never changed – those vast ovoid headlamps. These were adopted in the USA, too, in the final years.

(Above) *From this angle, and with the open-top body style chosen, there was no argument with the style of the XJ-S. After the model's resurgence in the 1980s, Jaguar's North American subsidiary positioned the car in the 'Go on, indulge yourself' category – and it shows!*

The vast stop/tail lamps of the original XJ-S would not be changed until 1991.

(Left) *By the end of the 1980s, the V12 engine bay had been tidied up considerably, but there was still a daunting amount of pipework, wiring and plumbing to terrify the home mechanic.*

(Below) *As other pictures make clear, the XJ-S shape only came together after years of trial, re-shaping and experiment. Looking good from this most flattering angle is a late-1970s model.*

Cabriolets were purely two-seater models, for instead of '+2' seating there was a neatly trimmed space for extra stowage.

(Above) *The 4.0-litre engined XJ-S was finally introduced into the USA in 1993, and was an immediate success. Before long it began to out-sell the 6.0-litre V12-engined version.*

(Above) *Although it looked good in the fully closed state, the cabriolet was really only a half-way attempt at providing XJ-S buyers with open-air motoring. As a two-seater coupé, though, it was an attractive proposition – do you like the 'no-flying-buttresses' effect?*

The cabriolet's roll-hoop was always prominent, clearly providing a great deal of extra body stiffness.

Hood down or …

… hood up, the convertible, launched in 1988, was a neater proposition than the cabriolet which it replaced.

(Right) The XJ-S was much bulkier than the E-Type, not only because it was built on a wider platform, but because it had a much longer 2+2 seater cabin.

(Left) The 'sail panels', or 'flying buttresses', were always a notable part of the design, which some people didn't like. But when Jaguar built prototypes without them, the result was found to be too bland.

(Right) XJ-S facias changed slowly, but significantly, over the years – gradually becoming more 'traditional Jaguar' with circular instruments, lots of wood and beautifully detailed leather trim.

Fifty years of Jaguar sporting heritage lined up, dramatically, to make a point about styling continuity. A late-1980s XJ-S convertible poses alongside an early-specification E-Type, an XK120 and an SS100.

To emphasize TWR's links with racing Jaguars, this publicity shot of the original XJR-S was taken at Silverstone, with the 1988 Le Mans winning Jaguar XJR-9 in the background.

At the same time, what a marketing department would call the 'customer profile' also changed. The average age of an XJ6 customer was fifty-two years, and that of an XJ-S owner forty-nine years. Jaguar-Sport's target was to change all that, to claw back some of the drivers who had defected to BMW or Porsche, and to bring back some of the sporting elements which had been present in the 1960s.

XJR-S – A FIVE-YEAR LIFE

The first new JaguarSport model was the XJR-S of August 1988, which was a lightly modified version of the TWR XJ-S V12 Coupé, which had already been a factory-approved conversion for some time. Priced at £38,500 (which compared with £32,900 for the standard XJ-S of the day), this car was badged to mark the TWR/Jaguar victory of 1988. It was nominated the Le Mans Celebration model, and the first one hundred apparently sold out very quickly indeed. These featured special paint and trim schemes (all were Tungsten Grey), victory laurels engraved on the treadplates on the door sills, and a plate showing the car's build number. Although the 5.3-litre engine and GM automatic transmission were not modified, there were important changes to the chassis, and to the styling.

Suspension changes included 11 per cent stiffer front springs, revalved Bilstein dampers at front and rear, a revalved

The original TWR-developed XJR-S of 1988 used the same engine as the standard XJ-S, but had suspension changes, wider-rim wheels and a body dress-up kit. Final assembly was at Kidlington, north of Oxford.

power-steering installation that actually gave less assistance, all allied to stiffer rack mountings and rear radius arm bushes.

New-style 7.5in rim Speedline alloy wheels and 235/60VR-15 Pirelli tyres added to the chassis changes, while style modifications included rather brutally detailed front and rear bumpers, along with a boot-lid spoiler.

To make these models, incomplete XJ-S Coupés (without bumpers, for instance) were assembled at Browns Lane before being transported forty miles to Kidlington. JaguarSport's fitters then finished off the car, tested the result, and delivered the complete machine direct to the chosen Jaguar dealer.

Naturally there had not yet been time to finalize any tune-up engine modifications. Accordingly, the first XJR-S was no faster than the standard car in a straight line, but justified itself by a firmer and more sporting ride/handling combination.

After the first 300 cars had been delivered, only a year later the next version of the XJR-S was ready, this time adding a more powerful 6-litre engine to modified versions of the original ride/handling/appearance package. Although this engine carried the same bore and stroke dimensions that the series-production XJ-S was to adopt from 1993, JaguarSport claimed to have done the development itself.

Not only was there a new long-stroke crankshaft (78.5mm instead of 70mm), but Zytek sequential injection, a digital ignition system and modified cold air intakes all helped raise the peak power to 318bhp at 5,250rpm. At the same time the wheel/tyre combination was enlarged still further – with 8.0 × 16in wheels and low-profile tyres (225/50 at the front, 245/55 at the rear), while yet another set of firmer springs – front and rear – were adopted.

Although JaguarSport sold the 6-litre XJR-S steadily, it was not quite the runaway success that had been hoped. Even

though limited exports – to Germany, France, Belgium, Holland, Italy and Spain – began in May 1990, the production rate steadily decreased. Jaguar's new owners, Ford, authorized the continuation of the XJR-S package on the facelifted car from 1991, though by that time cars were completed entirely at Browns Lane.

It was all in vain. Despite a further boost in peak power in the autumn of 1991, to a brawny 333bhp at 5,250rpm, and in spite of the speculative launch of an XJR-S convertible in the USA in 1992, this programme gradually ran down. The facelift car's price

TWR developed a 6-litre version of the V12 engine several years before it was ever adopted for use in mainstream Jaguars, using it in the final series of XJR-S types. Visually there were few differences, for the larger capacity was achieved by using the same cylinder bore and a longer stroke.

The last series of XJR-S models had 6.0-litre V12 engines, and were actually completed on the assembly line at Browns Lane. This is one of the rare 1991–93 re-styled examples, complete with re-shaped rear quarter window.

Jaguar XJR-S by JaguarSport (1988–93)

Layout

Based closely on the standard-production XJ-S, but with engine/suspension and trim changes by JaguarSport, based at Kidlington, Oxfordshire.

Compared with the standard car, these were the principal technical changes:

Engine

1988–89:	Standard specification
1989–91:	5,994cc (Bore and stroke 90 × 78.5mm)
	318bhp (DIN) @ 5,250rpm
	341lb.ft @ 3,750rpm
1991–93:	338bhp (DIN) @ 5,250rpm
	365lb.ft @ 3,650rpm

Suspension and steering

1988–89:	Tyres 235/60-15in, on wheels with 7.5in rim width
1989–93:	Tyres (front) 225/50-16in, (rear) 245/55-16in, on wheels with 8.0in rim width

---

was high: early in 1992 a 6-litre XJR-S retailed for £48,209, a colossal £6,382 more than the standard product. Ford, in any case, was known to be unimpressed by the style changes involved, and by the change to the production car's character. The XJR-S was finally withdrawn in 1993 when the mainstream 6-litre XJ-S appeared.

All in all, about 300 5.3-litre coupés and 500 6.0-litre cars (of which just fifty were USA-market convertibles) were produced. This did not mean the end for JaguarSport modifications, however, for these continued to be available to private customers.

By this time, in any case, Jaguar's latest six-cylinder engine had been added to the XJ-S range and the V12 was ready for retirement. A new generation of Jaguars, too, was on the way.

6 AJ6, Cabriolets and Convertibles

The XJSC of 1983 featured a cabriolet, rather than a true convertible, style, in which the window frames had been retained, along with a stout transverse roll-hoop. As seen here, this is as close to open-air motoring as the XJSC buyer could achieve.

Although the XJ-S Cabriolet appeared in 1983, at the same time as the new-generation AJ6 engine became an option in the car, the design of these two features was unconnected. The AJ6 engine, in fact, was a 'corporate' new design that had been on the go for some years – and was intended for use in every modern Jaguar in the 1980s – while the cabriolet body style only came into existence following pressure from customers and dealers, not least in the USA.

Well before the end of the 1970s, plans were being laid for a new family of six-

cylinder engines. By that time the design of the XK six-cylinder unit was more than thirty years old, and although it still looked magnificent – and was still being improved – it was nearing the end of its development. By modern standards the legendary XK engine was now heavy, low-revving, and thirsty: it was overdue for replacement.

For the 1980s and beyond, Jaguar set about developing a new 'straight six' engine family – one totally unconnected with the XK, that would be lighter, more fuel efficient, deeper breathing and more powerful than before. This engine was to be suitable for all current and planned Jaguars, notably the next-generation XJ6. However, after the second Energy Crisis of 1979 hit the XJ-S very hard indeed, attention also turned to matching the new engine to that car too.

SPEEDY DEVELOPMENT

As described in the panel (*see* page 105), the first new-generation six-cylinder engines were schemed up around V12 tooling, and several different layouts were investigated

before the first true prototype ran in 1979. By that time there were 12-valve single-overhead-cam and 24-valve twin-overhead-cam layouts, in 2.9-litre and 3.6-litre sizes, but for the XJ-S only the most powerful derivative, a 225bhp/24-valve/3.6-litre twin-cam type, was considered.

Jaguar were in no hurry to bring this engine to the market place, for it represented a very large capital investment for the future. It was, after all, only the third new engine family which the company had designed since 1945, and would need to be built for more than a decade to pay back that

Guess where and guess what? The XJ-S is a mid-1980s 3.6-litre six-cylinder engined coupé, the restaurant being one of many in the Le Mans area, in France, which makes sure you remember the famous 24-hour race!

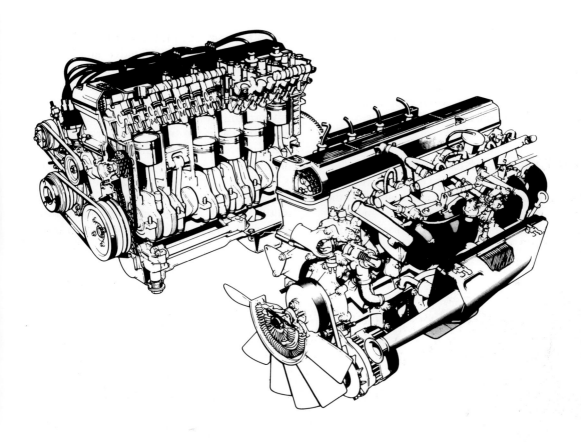

The new-generation AJ6 engine was developed in twin-cam (left) and single-cam (right) form, though it was only the twin-cam engine which was ever used in the XJ-S model.

investment in new tooling and facilities. Then, as later, AJ6 engines were machined at the Radford factory.

As ever with such an ambitious project, there were delays in bringing the engine to the public. Technically there was the challenge of meeting the latest (proposed) North American exhaust emission regulations, while suppliers had to grapple with the problem of supplying sturdy and accurate cast aluminium cylinder blocks and heads. This, after all, was the very first Jaguar engine to have four valves per cylinder, which ensured that the head castings were very complex indeed.

Then there was the question of finding the money to lay down the new plant. As mentioned earlier, Jaguar were losing a great deal of money at this stage, and had to petition their masters at the top of BL for funds. Michael Edwardes, though initially reluctant, was won round in the end:

When I went over the [Jaguar] engine plant at Radford in mid-1982, the stewards who accompanied the plant director, the head of Jaguar, John Egan and me showed a deep knowledge of the financial, commercial, productivity and manning implications of this new investment.

Because the XJ-S engine bay had been shaped around the massive bulk of the V12 engine, Jaguar engineers had very little difficulty in slotting the new-generation six-cylinder unit into the same space. Because its basic architecture – the bore spacings in particular – had slowly evolved from the 'half of a V12' layout, the new AJ6 was no longer than the V12, and although for installation reasons it was canted over at 15 degrees towards the exhaust side of the cylinder block, this was really a very comfortable installation. For the very first time on an XJ-S, mechanics actually found themselves with a few inches to spare to grovel

down around the sides of the cylinder block if necessary!

Technically this engine owed little to either of the older Jaguar designs, for apart from the four-valves-per-cylinder head layout and the aluminium cylinder block, the block had dry liners, a cast iron (instead of forged) crankshaft was used, and there was yet another modified type of fuel injection system.

More importantly, the new engine was much lighter than the old-type XK unit. At 430lb (195kg) in test-house condition it was no less than 21 per cent – one fifth – lighter, while it produced 11 per cent more power from 15 per cent smaller swept volume.

AJ6 ENGINE POWER AND TORQUE CURVES

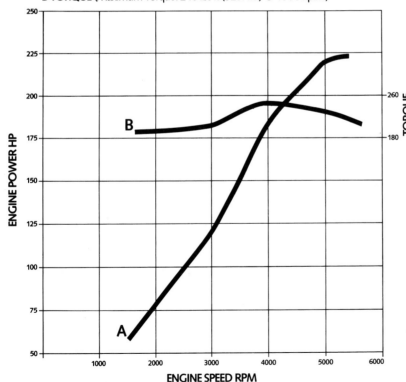

A POWER (Maximum Power: 225 bhp DIN (168kW) @ 5300 r.p.m.)
B TORQUE (Maximum Torque: 240 lbs ft (325Nm) @ 4000 r.p.m.)

The original AJ6 engine, in 3.6-litre twin-cam 24-valve form, developed 225bhp, with a very even torque curve.

The birth of the AJ6 six-cylinder engine

When the all-new AJ6 engine was unveiled in 1983, at first only for use in the XJ-S 3.6, the idea of a replacement for the gallant old XK six-cylinder engine had been slowly developing at Browns Lane for thirteen years. After the 3.5-litre V8 derivative of the new V12 had been abandoned in 1969/1970, no other layout than a straight-six was ever seriously considered.

First thoughts were of effectively using half of the new V12 engine as a 'slant-6', but this would only have been a 2.65-litre unit producing about 150bhp, though as we now know, larger displacement versions would also have been possible. After all, if TWR could go motor racing with 7-litre V12s, a 3.5-litre slant-6 would also have been feasible …

In fact a long-stroke version of the slant-6 was seriously considered, but the cylinder block could not then have been machined on the engine machining transfer lines at the Radford factory. It was time to think again. The idea of wedding a new 24-valve cylinder head to a modified XK bottom end was tried, then rejected, so in 1976 it was finally decided to take the 'Brave Pill' and start an all-new layout.

Harry Mundy led the project but Trevor Crisp, who took over from him in 1980, was always part of the project team. It was decided to develop 12-valve single-overhead-camshaft, and 24-valve twin-overhead-camshaft versions of the new layout. To give space around the engine in existing engine bays (particularly for the inlet manifolding and fuel injection), the new unit was designed to be canted over 15 degrees towards the near side of the engine bay. Although the XK had always used a cast iron cylinder block in production cars, in this case an aluminium alloy block was chosen instead. The new engine, incidentally, had a cast, rather than a forged, crankshaft.

The first prototypes ran in 1979, using cogged belt drive to the camshafts and auxiliaries, but duplex chains were later substituted, and there was even chain drive to the power-steering pump. There were no common components with the old XK design.

The first AJ6 to 'go public' was the 225bhp/3.6-litre XJ-S unit, while the 12-valve single-cam 165bhp/2.9-litre version was only used in the new-generation XJ6 of 1986.

Since that time, of course, development, improvement and enlargement of this engine family has continued. Not only were 4-litre versions soon readied, but supercharged versions were made available (both for the XJ6 and for the Aston Martin DB7), and it was the much-changed AJ16 version that powered the last of the XJ-S cars before the XK8 range arrived in 1996.

It was, in other words, exactly the right engine at the right time. Of equal importance to Jaguar was the fact that it could initially be produced in relatively small numbers for the latest XJ-S, almost as an extended pre-production exercise for use in the new-generation XJ6 saloon (XJ40) which was not due to go on sale until 1986.

Amid all the attention given to the new engine, and to the cabriolet body style that went with it, the arrival of a new manual transmission to back the engine (but not to back the V12) was sometimes ignored. Yet it was an important development, for 'stick-shift' V12s had always been very rare – and not available at all since 1979.

Originally there were to be two new 'building blocks', both German – a five-speed all-synchromesh manual gearbox from Getrag, and the modern ZF 4HP22 automatic transmission – but the ZF automatic was not available at first, so for the first three years all 3.6-litre engined cars were supplied with the manual transmission. Jaguar enthusiasts wondering if they could trust this new piece of kit were mollified when they learned that Getrag were long-time suppliers to BMW.

Jaguar XJ-S 3.6-Litre (1983–91)

Layout
Unit-construction steel body/chassis structure. Front engine/rear drive, sold as two-door, two-seater cabriolet from 1983–87, four-seater coupé from 1983–91.

Engine

Type	Jaguar AJ6, in-line six-cylinder
Block material	Cast aluminium
Head material	Cast aluminium
Cylinders	6, in-line
Cooling	Water
Bore and stroke	91×92mm
Capacity	3,590cc
Main bearings	7
Valves	4 per cylinder, operated by twin-overhead camshaft cylinder head, with inverted bucket-type tappets
Compression ratio	9.6:1
Fuel supply	Bosch-Lucas fuel injection
Max. power	228bhp (DIN) @ 5,300rpm
Max. torque	240lb.ft @ 4,000rpm

Transmission
Choice of manual or automatic transmissions.

Manual transmission: five-speed all-synchromesh Getrag gearbox.

Internal

Top	0.76:1
4th	1.00:1
3rd	1.39:1
2nd	2.06:1
1st	3.57:1
Reverse	3.46:1
Final drive ratio	3.54:1

Automatic transmission: four-speed ZF transmission, with torque converter.

Internal ratios

Direct	0.73:1
3rd	1.00:1
2nd	1.48:1

1st	2.48:1
Reverse	2.09:1
Maximum torque multiplication	2.0:1
Final drive ratio	3.54:1

Suspension and steering

Front	Independent, coil springs, wishbones, anti-roll bar, telescopic dampers
Rear	Independent, double coil springs, fixed length drive shafts, lower wishbones, radius arms, twin telescopic dampers
Steering	Rack-and-pinion, power-assisted
Tyres	(To 1988): 215/70VR-15in, radial-ply
	(From 1988): 235/60VR-15in, radial-ply
Wheels	Cast aluminium disc, bolt-on
Rim width	6.0in (6.5in from 1988)

Brakes

Type	Disc brakes at front and rear, with vacuum servo assistance
Size	11.8in diameter front, 10.40in diameter rear

Dimensions (in/mm)

Track	
Front	58.3/1,481
Rear	58.9/1,495
Wheelbase	102/2,591
Overall length	186.8/4,745
Overall width	70.6/1,793
Overall height	50.0/1,270
Unladen weight	Coupé 3,584lb/1,625kg
	Cabriolet 3,640lb/1,651kg
	Convertible 4,055lb/1,835kg

OPEN-TOP XJ-S – FIRST THOUGHTS

In the meantime, customer pressure for an open-top XJ-S had been growing rapidly, although such a car could only be justified if it could be sold in North America. Proposed US legislation that had threatened to render open-top cars illegal had long since been buried by public opinion, and several manufacturers had moved to fulfil a demand.

By the late 1970s, open-top cars were making a big comeback. Those like the MG MGB, the Fiat 124 Sport Spider, the Alfa Romeo Spider and the Mercedes-Benz SL had never been away, and continued to sell

The 3.6-litre engined XJ-S Coupé facia/instrument panel of the mid-1980s still retained the drum-type auxiliary instruments. This car, too, had the four-speed ZF automatic transmission.

strongly: from MG, for instance, it was the closed, not the drop-top, version of the MGB that had been withdrawn from the US market.

Way back, at the beginning of the 1970s, a convertible XJ-S (coded XJ28) had also been planned, but no serious work had ever been done on such a project. Now Jaguar customers who had always loved the E-Type Roadster were vocal – now that there were no legal difficulties they wanted an open-air XJ-S, and were not impressed by all the usual arguments about time, development problems, and capital spending.

Privately Jaguar's sales force and management agreed with them, but – as ever at

this time – they were bound by a lack of finance. Under Michael Edwardes, state-owned BL was currently throwing money at the Austin-Morris division, but rationing its development spending elsewhere. Although the open-top Triumph TR7 and TR8 sports cars came along in 1979, there was no sign of Jaguar following on.

Graham Whitehead nagged as much, and as often, as anyone else:

We got a lot of pressure from our dealers in the US, and Jaguar at Browns Lane had a fair amount of pressure from us. I think John Egan understood that the company needed a convertible.

John's first attempt was with the new cabriolet. I remember going to Browns Lane, and I think Mike Dale [Whitehead's sales chief] was with me. I think this was the only thing which John could do, at the time, it was very much his baby. He asked: 'Well, what do you think of it?'. I replied, 'Well, it's great, John, but it isn't a convertible.' He told us that for structural reasons it had to be like that, but it still wasn't a convertible. A good effort, but not yet far enough.

In the first months after he had arrived at Browns Lane, John Egan spent most of his time trying to keep the business alive. Once this had been achieved, so successfully, there is no doubt that he listened carefully to his dealers, concessionaires and customers.

As other company bosses found out to their cost at this time, his problem was technical rather than commercial. While there was no doubt that a big demand for open-top Jaguars existed, it was never going to be easy to develop an open version of the XJ-S.

Quite simply, and brutally, if the top was to be sliced off the XJ-S Coupé body shell, there was likely to be a catastrophic loss in torsional rigidity. The coupé that sat so solidly and reassuringly on the road – particularly on a rough road – might be turned into a convertible that wriggled and squirmed, vibrated and had serious scuttle shake problems.

A HALF-AND-HALF CAR

After a great deal of thought, therefore, Jaguar decided to produce a half-and-half car – a cabriolet instead of a true convertible. Even by Jaguar's own estimation there was a big difference between the two types, for a convertible, by definition, means a car whose top and sides can be completely stowed away, whereas the cabriolet has certain panels and sections that can be removed.

What this meant, in practical terms, was that although top panels could be removed from the reshaped cabin, a stout roll-over cage and solid body sides would remain in place to keep the torsional stiffness up to an acceptable level.

Looking back, I am sure that Jaguar always acknowledged that they would have to develop a full convertible one day, but that as an interim measure they would develop the openable-top cabriolet first. Not only that, but the cabriolet would only be a two-seater – not the 2+2 layout that had always been offered inside the coupé.

Although the platform of the XJ-S was unaffected, and the style was basically the same as ever, the cabin of the cabriolet was very different from that of the coupé. Although the windscreen, the doors, the tail, the boot lid and the rear wings were all substantially the same, almost everything above the waistline had to be new.

Most importantly, the sail panels linking the roof to the tail lamp area were abandoned. Solid steel pressings surrounded the top edges of the doors, and the reshaped quarter windows, linking the corners of the windscreen to the tonneau/shroud area immediately above the rear wheels, and these pressings were linked by a sturdy transverse 'roll cage' member, which acted as a brace between the pillars behind the doors.

From almost any angle, the cabin looked more squat than before, hid a formidable amount of new engineering, and gave the owner several driving options. Two fabric-covered interlocking panels ('Targa' panels – the name being borrowed from Porsche, who had reinvented this type of car in the mid-1960s) made up the removable roof section. When installed these made the car look like a fixed-head model with a fabric roof covering; when removed, these panels could be stowed in a storage envelope in the boot, or even left at home.

Behind the transverse roll-bar there was either a removable 'half hardtop' made from glass-fibre, with a glass rear window including a heating element, or in its place was a fold-up half-hood. The hood was always attached to the car, but when folded back lived below the rear deck line.

To accommodate the six-cylinder engine, by the way, there was a new bonnet pressing with a sleek 'power bulge' above the camshaft covers; although the engine was canted over in the engine bay, the power bulge was symmetrical. The only other obvious visual difference was that the SC used 'pepper-pot' alloy wheels (like those of the contemporary XJ6 saloon) instead of the 'Starfish' five-spokers of the V12-engined

XJ-S Coupé: since the 'Starfish' wheels were also optional, this often caused confusion among new-model spotters.

The upshot was that you could, if you wished, drive along in a snug saloon, in a saloon with the roof panels removed, in a semi-convertible with the roof panels and the rear 'hard-top/window' removed, or in further combinations of all these!

That this was not a viable long-term project became obvious when Jaguar revealed the way that the new cabriolet – the SC, as it was named – was to be assembled at first. Stage 1 for the XJ-SC started out with a standard body, pressed and partly assembled at the Jaguar body plant at Castle Bromwich (in the suburbs of Birmingham), though

The mid-1980s XJ-S, complete with 3.6-litre AJ6 engine, is identified by the road wheels and by the humped bonnet pressing.

The XJSC could be used in a variety of closed, open, or 'half-way open' states – here the car has had its roof panels removed, but the fold-back soft-top has been erected. The 'Starfish' wheels were optional extras when the new AJ6 six-cylinder engine was fitted.

some panels – notably the rear header panel and the roof – were omitted.

The incomplete shell was then transported to the Park Sheet Metal Co. in Coventry, for stage 2. The sail panels were removed, the underside was reinforced with a cruciform bracing, and the new-style upper side panels and the transverse brace were all added.

Stage 3 saw the completed shell trucked back to Castle Bromwich for painting. Stage 4 saw the shell trucked to Browns Lane for assembly of all mechanical components and trim. Stage 5 saw the near-complete car taken over to Aston Martin Tickford Ltd in Bedworth (north of Coventry) for the Targa panels and hood to be fitted, while stage 6

(the final stage) saw the car returned to Browns Lane for road test, sign off, and delivery to the customer.

No one, least of all Jaguar themselves, was totally happy with this method of building cars, which was very slow and difficult to achieve in numbers at first. To quote Jaguar-USA's John Dugdale:

You got the open-air feel and it had an ingenious pair of lift-out roof panels, but somehow it was not quite a convertible, and the convertible part was complex to fold and erect by hand. The sales force made the best of it, they were so relieved to have something to fill the product void ... The car was beautifully built, with its fully

---

The Tickford Connection

Tickford, the descendant of an independent coachbuilding concern at Newport Pagnell, was absorbed by Aston Martin in the 1950s. In the late 1970s a new consultancy business, Aston Martin Tickford Ltd, was set up, and began working for the British motor industry in many ways.

One important move was to take over an old factory in Bedworth, just north of Coventry, a building complex that had once made soft-tops for sports cars and convertibles and that was the right size to undertake batch production of special cars for manufacturers who could not cope with such limited numbers.

Among Tickford's most famous products were the speedy conversion of 500 Ford Sierra RS Cosworths into RS500 Cosworths, the building of MG Maestro and Rover 800 Turbos, production of soft-tops for 1990s-style Lotus Elans, British Rail coach interiors and the modernization and modification of many Ford RS200s before delivery.

Tickford, in fact, joined forces with Jaguar in the styling, design, development and manufacture of the 'convertible' aspect of the XJ-S Cabriolet. Tickford developed the system, after which it was also the pivot of a complex manufacturing process. First of all, from late 1983, normal XJ-S bodyshells, not quite complete, were produced at Jaguar's Castle Bromwich body shell plant, after which they were trucked to the Park Sheet Metal Co. in Coventry for conversion into 'body in white' cabriolet shells. They were then sent on to Jaguar for painting and mechanical assembly before being trucked, yet again, to Bedworth, where Tickford completed the Targa panels, the fold-away soft-top and other details.

At first, Jaguar could not cope with the finishing off of a cabriolet under their own roof at Browns Lane, but in due course the complexities of this procedure had to be tackled. In the winter of 1984–5 Jaguar took the completion job back 'in house', and Tickford played no further part in building these cars.

---

and padded convertible top, and some owners just loved them.

Although the 3.6-litre engine was available in cabriolet or coupé form, at this time there was no V12-cabriolet combination. The XJ-S product line, therefore, was by no means complete, while 1983/1984 sales were not helped by the extremely slow build-up of cabriolet deliveries in the first few months. Only 163 production cabriolets were built in 1983, followed by a mere 199 in the whole of 1984. This must surely have been due to the extraordinarily complex way of building cabriolets at first; although Park Sheet Metal continued to be involved in producing body shells, it was no surprise when Jaguar decided to take the whole assembly process back 'in house' in later years.

In many ways, the six-cylinder engine transplant had produced a very different type of XJ-S. It was still fast, but not as fast, still heavy, but not as heavy – though Jaguar thought it was now an ideal 'entry level' to this class of car. Subtle changes to the suspension and chassis settings had made the car slightly more sporting – less of a limousine – which went well with the open-top character.

Press Reactions

Like several other groups of testers, my old colleagues on *Autocar* were quite clear about the SC's merits. They liked the all the usual 'Jaguarness', which included surprisingly high performance, good ride quality, low noise levels and the obvious value for

Yet another slight variation of 1980s-style XJ-S interiors, this actually being a 1987-model six-cylinder engined model, complete with the Getrag manual transmission. At this stage, elm rather than walnut, was still used for wood veneer.

money, but they were not happy with the Getrag gearbox's change quality and the jerkiness of the engine/drive-line combination: this last, if it was present in V12-

engined cars, was presumably concealed by the smoothing action of the torque converter and the automatic transmission.

Although there was a loss of performance

compared with the V12 cars, the XJ-SC was still a very quick car. This is how the basic statistics compared:

	XJ-SC 3.6-litre	XJ-S HE V12 5.3-litre
Engine size (cc)	3,590	5,343
Brake horse power	225	299
Unladen weight (lb)	3,577	3,824
Maximum speed (mph)	141	153
0–60mph (sec)	7.4	6.5
0–100mph (sec)	19.7	15.7
Standing-start ¼-mile (sec)	15.9	14.9
Typical fuel consumption (mpg – Imperial)	19/20	17/18

Autocar testers commented:

Judged with or without reference to the V12 model, the XJ-S is a most refined grand touring car ... Conversation with only slightly raised voices is possible at the maximum speed and the car is marvellously quiet and relaxed at any normal cruising speed. As ever, perhaps the most impressive feature of the XJ-S is its ride ...

With the performance merely 'as expected' – in fact the XJ-SC was as quick in a straight line as the last of the E-Type 2+2s, which were smaller and had a larger engine – testers' emphasis was on character, and not on statistics. The summary told its own story:

Even taking into account its old-fashioned and undistinguished instrument styling ...

Wall-to-wall AJ6 engines, as manufactured at the Radford factory.

it so clearly still offers the best blend of qualities for the price; superb noise refinement and ride, with good handling, largely effortless performance, competitive levels of economy for the class, and air conditioning. Even taking the faults into account, it remains a hard act for the others to follow.

Even so, this was not an XJ-S derivative that Jaguar thought it could sell in the USA. Graham Whitehead (and, later, his successor Mike Dale) liked to keep Jaguar's model-line simple, so for the next two years the only cars delivered in Jaguar's biggest single export market were the XJ6 saloons and the V12-engined XJ-S; from 1986 the V12-engined XJ-SC was added to that line-up, but six-cylinder XJ-S types would not arrive in the USA in numbers until 1993. To quote Whitehead:

I think that people were buying the XJ-S because of its performance, it was the top of the line. There didn't seem to us to be a demand, or a need, for the six-cylinder car. According to our market research, sales would have been 'substitutional' – and probably substitutional at a lower profit margin. There was always an underlying marketing strength in that V12.

Accordingly, deliveries of the AJ6-engined XJ-SC built up slowly, the specification gradually changing to offer more options. After the V12-engined version appeared in mid-1985 (as mentioned in the previous chapter), cosmetic changes were made to the interior of the car at the 1985 London Motor Show.

PRODUCTION CHANGES

There was more to come. From February 1987 not only were more facia/switchgear/centre console changes introduced across the range, but the four-speed ZF Type 4HP22 automatic transmission was finally made available, and at the same time significant changes were made to the engine, its detail construction, and not least to its fuel injection control – all a result of three years' further development that had been put in for the new-generation XJ6, which had finally gone on sale. What with the arrival of the new XJ6, and the engineering department's move to Whitley, there was so much going on at Jaguar in 1987 that the passing of two milestones – the building of the 100,000th V12 engine, and of the 50,000th XJ-S – passed unnoticed.

Then, from September 1987, Jaguar offered a '3.6 Sportspack' option, which aimed to make the six-cylinder engined car feel even more sporting and less 'boulevard cruiser' than the V12 or the standard model. The Sportspack was a thorough reworking of the chassis settings, for there were fatter 235/60-section tyres on wider (6.5in rim) wheels, a 'quicker' steering rack, much firmer front suspensions, rerated dampers all round, and a reintroduced rear anti-roll bar.

THE HESS & EISENHARDT CONVERTIBLE

By the mid-1980s the pressure for an open-top XJ-S had become unstoppable. In the USA one problem was that most customers were avid readers of European motoring magazines, had noted the announcement of the XJ-SC, but then found that it was not to be sold in North America.

Even after the V12 version of the SC appeared in the UK – in July 1985 – there was a nine-month delay before it officially went on sale in North America. Almost immediately after that, USA dealers found the same customer resistance to the rigid sides and the roll-bar that Jaguar had discovered in the UK. Mike Cook, who had been obliged to field all the 'coupé-only' comments for years, and try to turn it to Jaguar's advantage, sums up what happened next:

The demand for a full convertible started as soon as the XJ-S came over here [to the USA]. The dealers wanted it, badly. As John Egan began to revive the company, and began to lead it back out of the depths, the demand began again.

But we were still on a long product cycle. There we were in 1983 and 1984 saying that we had to have a convertible, otherwise XJ-S sales were going to sit where they were. Jaguar actually started developing the proper convertible in 1985, and said:

'Well, we can give you a convertible in 1988 or 1989' – but we couldn't wait that long.

This was the point at which Jaguar's Mike Dale started looking round for a specialist in the USA to do the job for him – and very rapidly, too. At that time the coach-building industry in the USA was strong, so after a great deal of research a Cincinnati-based concern, Hess & Eisenhardt, was chosen to do the job: 'Actually it was a coincidence,' Mike Cook says, 'but I already knew a lot about H & E, because I went to school with one of the Hess family in Cincinatti.' Hess & Eisenhardt were a solid, custom-body company, which had started by building horse-drawn carriages in 1876, had

Well before Jaguar could prepare its own full convertible, Jaguar Cars Inc. sponsored this American-made conversion from Hess & Eisenhardt of Cincinatti, Ohio. The easy way to 'pick' this car from the factory convertible is to note the more bulky screen surround and header rail.

built many Buick and Cadillac convertibles, and whose regular product was Cadillac stretch limousines. They had the facilities and the capability to engineer an XJ-S Convertible from the top down – literally – and to build them in numbers: to H & E this was normal business.

Jaguar-USA announced a co-operative deal in January 1986, and the first deliveries were made later in the year, the new derivative only being available in the USA: as far as I know, no example was ever sold in the UK. Initially this was an eighteen-month contract. The demand surprised everyone, not least H & E, who had to concentrate on the Jaguar project to the virtual exclusion of every other project for a time!

Before Jaguar's own XJ-S Convertible took over in the USA in 1988, about 2,000 units were produced.

Commercially and practically, this was always a complex deal. This was an officially recognized car, with a dual warranty, with Jaguar continuing to back all 'their' bits, and with H & E backing the details of the special conversion.

Cars were not available from stock. A customer would go to his dealer, sort out his choice of colour, then order an H & E Convertible. The dealer placed an order for an XJ-S Coupé to be shipped to Cincinnati. H & E carried out the conversion, shipped the car to the dealer, and the customer eventually got his hands on a car. By North American

The Hess & Eisenhardt conversion of 1986–88 was only sold through Jaguar dealers in the USA, and was a very successful stop-gap car before the factory model became available.

'I want it now' standards, the patience needed was extraordinary, though the work was usually completed in about four weeks.

To produce this carefully jig-built model, H & E would strip out a car, carve off the roof and sail panels, stiffen up the main sills, A-posts, and crossmember/heelboard under the occasional rear seats, then weld new tonneau and upper rear wing panels into place.

Once repainted (only the top and rear of the car, not the entire shell), the modified car would then get its electrically operated soft top, which, when folded back, lived under a rather large leather pouch. Compared with the existing coupé, incidentally, there were no occasional rear seats, and there was a redesigned double fuel tank arrangement.

Although the 1986 retail price of a H & E Convertible was no less than $47,000, this was backed by a 36-month/36,000 mile warranty, so there was a healthy demand for this individual model. By any specialist standards this was a successful model, though certain features clearly did not appeal to Jaguar, who did not repeat them on the factory convertible.

The most important failing was that there seemed to be persistent leakages from the twin fuel-tank arrangement, which caused smells, and while H & E clearly did their craftsmanlike best with the conversion and repainting, there tended to be mid-life problems with bubbling and blistering of the paintwork.

No doubt if a lot more time had been available, too, H & E would have been able to reduce what the Americans call the 'stack height' – the amount by which the folded-back soft-top protruded above the line of the rear deck – which somehow did not seem to match the high sticker price.

By the late 1990s the 'classic' value of these cars had dropped to between $12,000 and $15,000. One problem was that H & E had hit serious financial problems by the end of the 1980s, and had not always honoured their warranty on the car, which meant that the cars tended to deteriorate somewhat in the hands of a third or even a fourth owner.

A Real Convertible at Last

In the meantime, Jaguar management had finally found the time, the workforce and the man-hours to develop their own full convertible, a car that they intended to be cheaper and available in much larger quantities, than the largely craftsman-carved cabriolet. As work on the new-generation XJ6 passed its peak, body specialists could then turn their attention to the XJ-S once again – but even so, extra consultancy help was needed to finish the job.

Although work on Jaguar's own XJ-S Convertible began in May 1985, when we know that the project team was initially only twelve people, the production car was not ready for launch until March 1988, the actual debut being at the Geneva Show. In the meantime, the cabriolet project was gradually run down, with the last of the six-cylinder cars being built in September 1987, and the last of all – a V12 version – following in February 1988.

Compared with the cabriolet, the XJ-S Convertible not only looked different, but was structurally very different too. Jaguar – and Karmann, their German consultants – had been faced with the usual problem: how to cut off the roof of a monocoque while retaining sufficient torsional stiffness in the shell. This was much more difficult with the convertible than with the cabriolet, which had, at least, retained a skeleton of steel around the removable panels and the fold-back rear section. For the new convertible, for styling reasons, there could be no steel stiffeners above the waistline, or aft of the screen rail.

This was the Real Thing – Jaguar's own XJ-S Convertible, which was introduced in 1988 and soon became the best-selling model in the range. Like the Cabriolet it replaced, it was only a two-seater.

Although the XJ-S Coupé was heavy and had an extremely rigid body shell, much of that strength disappeared when the roof and sail panels were cut off. Jaguar knew what had to be done – extra stiffening panels would have to be used and bracing would have to be applied to the floorpan and pillars – but to make doubly sure of the result the company called on Karmann, an independent concern that had a formidable reputation in this type of engineering.

Although German, Karmann were well known to the British motor industry – and to motoring enthusiasts all round the world. Not only were Karmann famous for building huge numbers of cars, but for being experts in soft-top development, and the tooling up of limited-production bodywork.

Karmann had not only made VW Karmann-Ghia coupés, but styled and tooled-up the Triumph TR6, and were the VW-contracted builder of every Golf Convertible, and were carrying out much work for Porsche and BMW and for the Ford Escort Cabriolet. With the possible exception of Pininfarina, no other European coachbuilder was as well qualified.

As with the cabriolet, which the convertible would oust, the intention was to make this a two-seater with a large lockable compartment behind the seats. Unlike the Hess & Eisenhardt conversion (which the Coventry team did not see until its own design job was complete), there were to be a more elegant screen and surround panels, though the soft-top still stood several inches proud of the rear deck level when folded back.

To stiffen up the open-top shell, many new panels and a great deal of modification was needed to the underpan. By the time the work was done, Jaguar admitted that one third of the panels were new or substantially modified. All in all, there were 108 new panels, and 48 modified ones.

Much work had gone into firming up the front and rear bulkheads, the sills, the A-posts (door posts), the sills, the transmission tunnel and the rear floor. Karmann's expertise also led to the addition of stout steel tubes inside the sills and the A-posts,

and at all times the aim was to make the shell stiff without losing any of the car's renowned refinement.

Amazingly, too, Jaguar had to take advice on the design of the electrically operated soft top, for the last all-Jaguar soft top had been designed for the E-Type in 1958/1959 – and that had not needed any power assistance. The final product, a complex fold-back mechanism that could be raised or lowered in a mere 12 seconds, was a framed fabric top with a rigid glass rear window, complete with tinting and a heating element.

Even with the soft-top erect, the XJ-S Convertible was still an elegant car, and rearward visibility was surprisingly good.

The new car, which would only be available with the V12 engine at first, went into production in the spring of 1988, at the same time as yet another package of chassis changes were also phased in. From this time the car got Teves-type ABS anti-lock brakes, modified front and rear suspension components, and a new style of 6.5in rim lattice alloy road wheel with Pirelli P600 tyres.

This time the new open-top Jaguar took shape in a straightforward way, and there was no question of 'knife-and-fork' constructional methods. Every panel in the shell was pressed at the Castle Bromwich body plant, where body shell assembly and painting were also carried out, and the remainder of assembly – in particular the erection of the soft-top – was completed at Browns Lane.

Castle Bromwich – the body and pressings plant

Jaguar's Castle Bromwich body plant has had a complex history, yet has only been dedicated to the building of Jaguar body shells since the 1980s. By the end of the 1990s, though, it was also due to house new facilities for the complete manufacture and assembly of a new generation of smaller Jaguar cars.

Before the 1980s, Jaguar had never had its own body supply plant: ever since the Mk VII was launched in 1950, its saloon shells, later monocoques, had been sourced from the Pressed Steel (later Pressed Steel Fisher) Co. Ltd factories at Cowley, and later from Swindon.

Although the Castle Bromwich factory is only five miles north-east of the centre of Birmingham, alongside the A452, and very close to Junction 5 of the M6 motorway, the site overlooked green fields until the 1940s. The first buildings on this site were erected by the Nuffield Organisation, as a 'shadow' factory for military aircraft production. Building work began in 1938, and the plant was ready to start producing Spitfires in 1940. Then, after a blazing row between Lord Nuffield and Lord Beaverbrook, the plant was reallocated to Vickers Armstrong.

During World War Two the plant expanded enormously, eventually building 12,000 Spitfires and 300 Lancasters, the area on the other side of the road being Castle Bromwich airfield where all flight test operations took place. After the war this massive plant was then taken over by Fisher & Ludlow, which was then an independent body-making concern.

A series of mergers then followed. F & L were absorbed by BMC in 1953, became a part of Pressed Steel Fisher in the 1960s, and after 1968 were soon almost submerged into the mass of British Leyland. Up to that time, 'the Fisher' factory concentrated on building bodies and monocoques for BMC, including Minis, Austin A50 Cambridges, and many 1960s BMC cars.

By the end of the 1970s, however, a reshuffle within Pressed Steel Fisher resulted in the stamping and assembly of Jaguar body shells being moved from Cowley and Swindon to the Castle Bromwich site.

By the time that Jaguar was privatized in 1984, the Castle Bromwich workforce was concerned only with the assembly and painting of Jaguar monocoques – these being the XJ6/XJ12 and XJ-S units. By no means was all of the site fully occupied (which made the short-lived setting up of a pressings venture with GKN, at Telford, rather difficult to understand), which explains why Ford, who had owned Jaguar from 1989, were so ready to clear some of it, and to build a brand-new assembly plant for the next generation of 'small' Jaguars in the late 1990s.

From the very beginning, XJ-S monocoques were always pressed and assembled at Castle Bromwich, the same buildings also supplying incomplete shells to specialist firms in Coventry to build the XJ-S Cabriolet version – and also supplying modified platforms to Motor Panels Ltd of Coventry so that Aston Martin DB7 Coupé and Volante shells could also take shape.

Naturally, the late 1990s XK8 shells were also produced at Castle Bromwich.

The various statistics were impressive. Complete with its new ABS braking, the new XJ-S Convertible weighed 20lb/9kg more than the coupé, yet the aerodynamic shape (with hood erect) was so good that the claimed top speed was still 150mph (240km/h). In 1988 the last of the V12 cabriolets had been listed at £31,000, while by mid-summer 1988 the first of the F-registered convertibles was priced at £38,500 – a whopping 24 per cent price rise.

REBIRTH OF THE XJ-S

When the XJ-S Convertible finally went on sale, it was almost as if Jaguar had touched a trigger. The company's reputation, already booming again as the 1980s stock market booms neared their peaks, leapt yet again. Road testers were enthusiastic, customers flocked to the showrooms and sales surged ahead. Except for the few who continued to call the car too large, too heavy, too thirsty, and not pretty enough, tens of thousands of rich people chose an XJ-S in the late 1980s – often for the second or even the third time.

To make the point again, it is worth summarizing (*see* box below) how the XJ-S prospered, particularly in North America.

For a car that had been conceived early in the 1970s and that had been on sale for well over a decade, this surge was remarkable. In 1989 *ten times* as many XJ-S cars were produced as had been built in 1980, all from the same assembly lines in Coventry, which had received no investment in that time. It was no wonder that the privatized Jaguar concern was now attracting attention from predators, and why the stock market price reached unprecedented heights.

Over in the USA, the Hess & Eisenhardt conversion was phased out as soon as the factory version became available, but Mike Cook recalls that very little promotion, or explanation, was ever needed:

There hadn't actually been a great deal of promotion for the H & E Convertible, not nationally, not in terms of advertising. It was just something which the dealers had available.

But as soon as the factory convertible appeared, it was a huge success. Fortunately we were able to counter the 'Why didn't you do this ten years ago?' remarks with reminders about British Leyland's past, and the USA legislation proposals. We just said we'd done our best, here it was, and you really could buy it now!

	XJ-S production in the late 1980s		
Year	**XJ-S production**	**XJ-S sales in the USA**	**USA market comment**
1985	7,951	3,784	V12 coupé still the only US model
1986	9,052	4,885	First deliveries of V12 cabriolet
1987	9,826	5,380	Three V12 models: coupé, cabriolet, H & E Convertible
1988	10,356	4,783	Factory convertible introduced
1989	11,207	4,458	Convertible took 57 per cent of sales.

The new XJ-S Convertible of 1988 was an immediate success, especially in the USA, where this four-headlamp car was sold.

The new convertible was a big success – a major success. It didn't kill the coupé – there were still people wanting an XJ-S with a roof – but it started outselling it almost at once. It was a great car for the dealers, because they didn't have to carry a whole load of extra parts, because the basic chassis was the same.

North American testers were ecstatic. When *Road & Track* first saw the car, the writer reminded his readers that the obsolete XJ-SC was:

> ... a skeletal-framed cabriolet open to both air and aesthetic criticism ...

but that the new car had

> ... a very rigid chassis with excellent torsional strength and body structure. The con-

vertible's ride and handling characteristics were certainly up to Jaguar snuff.

The full road test followed later (and was actually published in the January 1989 issue). Headlined 'The Return of the Midsummer Night's Dream', the test made all the points that were bound to please Jaguar Cars Inc.:

> This is a luxury car rather than a sports car. It's a marvellously relaxing car to drive a long distance at a fast pace because it always feels as if it has enough of everything – enough roadholding for a mountain drive, enough power for the uphill pass and enough comfort that you won't be dismayed if the traffic slows down and you get there a little late. After all, the inside of an XJ-S is a nice place to be.

Even though the North American specification cars were rather less powerful than those sold in the UK – *R & T*'s car boasted 262bhp at 5,000rpm – they still had formidable performance. With a top speed of 141mph (227km/h), a 0–60 speed of 9.9 seconds, and an overall 'gas mileage' of 13 USA mpg (22l/100km), this prompted the remark that:

> From rest to well past 100mph, the sense of unbroken acceleration reminds one of being lifted 40 floors in a fast elevator …

Autocar's car, in standard (291bhp) 'rest-of-the-world' tune, was significantly faster, and more economical. It took only 8.0 seconds to reach 60mph, the top speed was 144mph (232km/h), and overall returned

13.8 Imperial mpg (20.5l/100km). It was no wonder that the testers wrote:

> The E-Type is dead, long live the XJ-S Convertible. Fresh-air fiends can once more indulge their passion in the grand style and enjoy Jaguar's V12 performance and handling to match.

Improved quality and more complete testing were both mentioned, including:

> To ensure longevity, Jaguar has put the hood and mechanism through rigorous testing, which included raising and lowering the hood 8,000 times – the equivalent of one hood operation a day for 22 years. Jaguar engineers have also made the hood operation idiot-proof. It cannot be operated

This was the 'Le Mans Celebration' limited-edition version of the XJ-S V12 Coupé, which was marketed in 1990 just before the major restyle. Note the four-headlamp nose, not previously available in the UK.

In 1990 the XJ-S range was at the height of its popularity – this trio covering the six-cylinder (top right) and V12 types, open and closed.

unless the handbrake is on, and the gear selector is in Park.

The summary spelt out the way in which Jaguar had redeemed itself with the often-cynical motoring press:

Three years of intense development and attention to detail have really paid off for Jaguar. The XJ-S V12 Convertible is a very complete and accomplished tourer in the true sense of the word. It is capable of taking two people and luggage over long distances in great comfort. At £36,000 [the launch price, soon raised] it may be the most expensive production Jaguar to date, but we feel it is worth every penny.

At this stage, amazingly, Jaguar did not mate the new convertible body style with the 3.6-litre engine, which meant that the engine that had ushered in XJ-S open-air motoring in 1983 was now only available in a coupé again: the open-top 'six' version would not reappear, in fact, until 1992.

TAKE-OVER BY FORD

Although the XJ-S looked set-fair for the next few years, all manner of corporate and financial undercurrents then elbowed the car out of the limelight. By 1989 the first sneak pictures of a prototype Jaguar popularly dubbed 'the F-Type' were published,

125

Sir John Egan (born 1939)

When John Egan arrived at Jaguar in 1980, the company was virtually on its knees. The assembly lines were at a standstill, the marque's quality reputation was in tatters, and it was not expected to survive for long.

In 1980 the company lost £46 million, built a mere 14,000 cars, and for a time actually withdrew the XJ-S from the market completely. Six years later, production had rocketed to 43,000 cars and profits were running at £122 million a year. Not only that, but the company had successfully been split off from British Leyland, and had been privatized: the Stock Market, and investors, loved every minute of this. Much, if not all, of that improvement was credited to the dynamism and leadership given to the company by Egan, who was knighted for his efforts in the Birthday Honours list of 1986.

Before joining Jaguar, Sir John had completed impressive spells with BL's Unipart division, and with Massey Ferguson. At Jaguar he had an uphill struggle at first, not least in convincing unions and suppliers that he would close down the business if quality and labour relations did not improve: as a result he turned the business around. Helped along by inventive and vigorous public relations activity, he also convinced the world (particularly in North America) that Jaguar was on the way back.

At first he was Jaguar's chief executive, reporting to Ray Horrocks at BL cars, and for a short time after privatization in 1984 he retained that position under the chairmanship of Hamish Orr-Ewing; after Orr-Ewing stood down in March 1985, Egan became the undisputed boss of Jaguar. Not only did he bring the new AJ6 engine to the market (it powered the XJ-S before any other models), but he also master-minded the evolution of the new-generation XJ6 (the XJ40 project), which reached the public in 1986, oversaw the purchase and redevelopment of the Whitley design/engineering centre, and, most important of all for the sporting enthusiasts, he supported Tom Walkinshaw's enterprise in its motor racing programme.

Until 1988, in fact, he kept every possible corporate ball in the air, but once the long drawn-out negotiations with General Motors stalled, and the forced sale to Ford had been agreed in 1989, it was clear that he would soon be stepping down. His resignation became effective in June 1990 (when Ford nominee Bill Hayden took his place), after which he moved on to control BAA, the British Airports Authority.

In future years, Jaguar enthusiasts may wonder why Sir John took no interest in Jaguar after he had left – he refused to be interviewed when this book was being prepared – and there is mounting evidence to suggest that he was more of a businessman than a car enthusiast throughout his tenure at Browns Lane. No matter – without his efforts, Jaguar might have disappeared in the early 1980s.

---

and a long-running battle resulted in Jaguar losing their hard-won independence once again, this time to Ford.

Ford, like Jaguar, had been in the doldrums early in the 1980s, but by 1989 it was eagerly looking for acquisitions, large and small. Successes included the purchase of Aston Martin and AC (both, according to Ford's ever-quotable Walter Hayes, for 'petty cash'), though failures included an attempt to buy Austin-Rover and Alfa Romeo (shot down by Italian politics and Fiat).

In 1989, however, Ford's eyes turned towards Jaguar – though not before they had been goaded into this by a similar interest shown by their deadly rival, General Motors. Sir John Egan, we now know, had started looking round for a partner in March 1988, for it was becoming clear that Jaguar, on their own, could not finance all the new models and facilities that they needed to secure the 1990s and beyond.

For Jaguar, and for the XJ-S, the implications were enormous.

7   The Long Goodbye –
1991 to 1996

If Ford had not taken over Jaguar when they did, there might never have been a successor to the XJ-S, nor even a facelift for the existing model. Jaguar, in fact, might not have survived. By 1989, in truth, Jaguar's profits were melting away rapidly and questions were already being raised about the company's long-term survival.

Although the engineers and designers working away on improvements to all the cars – not least the XJ-S – had to assume that capital would always be found to fund these changes, they must have realized that their company might hit trouble before this could be done.

Even though most of them had been tied up with the new-generation XJ6, the V12 version of that car – and the move to a new home at Whitley – for some time, there had still been a little breathing space to keep up with the XJ-S. At the time Jaguar's strategy was to design a brand-new sporting car, maybe with four-wheel-drive, but as this would take years, there was still thought to be scope to introduce one final batch of changes to the XJ-S.

Customers, dealers and concessionaires seemed to be happy with the chassis and running gear – the performance, the ride and the general handling package were still at the very top of the Super Coupé league – so it was tacitly agreed that most of the changes should concentrate on the styling.

Doug Thorpe, who took over as Jaguar's styling director after Sir William Lyons retired in the 1970s, always admitted to being uneasy about the flying-buttress feature on the first XJ-S, whose shape had been 'frozen' when he settled into the new job. Over the years, however, the original style persisted. By the mid-1980s there was time (and, potentially, some money) for changes to be made but every effort, however serious, was eventually abandoned. One such attempt, carried out in 1984 after the cabriolet had gone on sale, was not just a redesign to eliminate the sail panels/buttresses, but also set out to provide a larger cabin and more rear-seat/leg-room.

Although this was undoubtedly a more practical car than before, problems remained. In spite of all stylist Geoff Lawson's packaging efforts, this was still a 2+2 rather than a four-seater, and the tooling bill for a carve-up that included yet more new floor pressings was too costly. Not only that, but the full convertible, which followed, might not have been compatible with the lengthened wheelbase.

By the late 1980s attention had turned to a major facelift of the existing car, which would retain the same floorpan and running gear, and most of the existing panels. Any reshaping proposed would have to be suitable for use on the closed and open versions – for it was already clear that the convertible was going to be dominant in the XJ-S's final years.

There was, however, one major snag. Although the stylists soon agreed on what

---

The Whitley Technical Centre

Like many other industrial buildings in Coventry, the Whitley facility was originally built with military production in mind, the area having been used as a grass airfield since 1918. When first built, to the south-east of Coventry's city centre, it was well clear of any housing (and was therefore very secure), was used for aircraft testing in the 1920s, and later (after the first major buildings were erected) for aircraft component manufacture by the Armstrong-Whitworth business. By the end of the 1930s, suburbia had arrived on its boundaries, and was only kept at bay by the building of the Coventry eastern by-pass in the 1970s, which separates the factory from the city itself.

Much of the Whitley bomber was assembled there during the 1930s and 1940s, but from 1948 onwards it was used exclusively for guided weapons development. By the 1960s, however, the site was deserted, so in 1969 it was sold off to the Rootes Group (which had recently been taken over by Chrysler of the USA). Rootes-Chrysler then redeveloped it as a motor vehicle design and development technical centre, concentrating all its new-model work at Whitley from 1970.

After Chrysler sold out to Peugeot in 1978, Whitley was controlled by Peugeot-Talbot Ltd., but that company then gradually ran down its new-car design facilities, finally pulling out of Whitley and selling it on to Jaguar in 1985.

Jaguar then completely re-equipped the 155-acre site, built a sparkling new-style façade, erected several new buildings, made space for 1,000 engineers and their high-tech. equipment, and admitted to spending £55 million on the project. Technical staff began moving from Browns Lane to Whitley in 1987 and 1988, the complex being officially opened in May 1988.

Although XJ-S work was initially carried out at Browns Lane in the 1970s and 1980s, design and development work on the facelifted cars revealed in 1991 was completed at Whitley, as was the entire concept, design, development and proving of the XK8 which took over from the XJ-S in 1996.

---

should be done, where the new panels would have to fit to the existing pressings, how long this would take to develop, and at what cost – the money was simply not available. If Ford had not come along to underpin Jaguar's future in 1989, the reshaped XJ-S would never have appeared.

FORD TO THE RESCUE

By mid-1989 the City of London was openly talking about a future take-over battle for Jaguar, and in the autumn events moved swiftly. In September, Jaguar announced a profits collapse for the first half of the year – from £22.5 million in 1988 to a mere £1.4 million in 1989. Almost at the same time, Ford announced their intention to buy a stake in Jaguar. Prime Minister Margaret Thatcher endorsed this as good for the company – and it became clear that Ford's major rival, General Motors, was also drawing up a financial proposal. Graham Whitehead commented:

> I suppose there was some trepidation at the time. As I was on the parent board it was quite obvious that Jaguar could not last long on its own.

Yet there were major differences between the two proposals. GM, which had been moving slowly forward with John Egan's encouragement, merely wanted to take a minority stake, and to offer a gradual approach towards integration. Ford, on the other hand, wanted to take complete financial control, to provide some of the company's top managers, systems, and purchasing power, and not only

Although the visual effects of the restyle of 1991 concentrated on the new side-window profile and the new tail lamps, Jaguar claimed that more than one third of the panels were new. There's little evidence of such change from this view

aimed to turn round Jaguar but to expand it, without erasing its character: Jaguar, which is to say John Egan, did not favour a complete take-over. When Ford declared their intent, Jaguar's shares rose sharply, making their stock-market value worth more than £1 billion, but Jaguar were not impressed. At this time Jaguar spokesman David Boole commented publicly:

> We do not welcome Ford's approach. We want to remain independent and we feel that's the best way to serve the interests of our shareholders and customers.

By this time, though, there was no turning back, and a full-scale take-over battle soon developed. First of all GM announced that they were 'close to a deal', yet that they would only buy 15 per cent of the capital, rising to 30 per cent when the government's 'Golden Share' time-limit expired at the end of 1990.

Ford, who history will show moved much faster than GM, then speedily bought 12 per cent of the shares for £140 million, instead of just talking about it. The government than stated that it was withdrawing the 'Golden Share' limitation. Immediately,

Ford offered £8.50 per share for the entire capital, thus making what the City called a 'knock-out' bid, worth a colossal £1.6 billion: since 1984, therefore, the shares had rocketed in value from £1.65 to £8.50 – a rise of 515 per cent. If John Egan had proposed to walk on water at that moment, the shareholders would have been ready to believe him!

Ford – saviour or predator?

For the first few years after privatization, Jaguar's future looked to be set fair. By 1989, as described in the main text, all the indicators were pointing the wrong way, and Sir John Egan was happy to look around for a partner.

In the end, the battle was between two North American giants – Ford and General Motors – the contest eventually being won because Ford was decisive while GM dithered. Some financial observers suggest that Ford paid far too much for Jaguar, but the fact is that that price included the immeasurable goodwill of a truly charismatic name.

Fortunately for Jaguar enthusiasts, Ford never committed any of the sins which the doom-mongers suggested would follow. There was no instant 'badge-engineering', and no dilution of the 'Jaguarness' of the cars. As the 1990s developed, Ford not only paid all the bills and stemmed the losses, but financed the development of the much-changed 1991-variety XJ-S, followed it up with approval for the latest-generation XJ6 range of saloons, then committed huge amounts of capital investment for the new-generation V8 engine and the XK8 range to be put on sale.

Happily for all Jaguar enthusiasts, the marque's future was safe with Ford, and all the signs were that great things were planned for the first years of the 21st century.

John Egan later confirmed that he had given GM two weeks notice of Ford's impending 100 per cent bid, but that the corporation did not react:

Because they decided they wouldn't pay £1.6 billion. By then Ford was looking the better owner. They were more positive about the whole thing... Our discussions with GM didn't always go well.

The take-over was formalized in November, and by the end of the year Jaguar had become a wholly-owned subsidiary of Ford. At first it was Ford-of-Europe that controlled the business, but for administrative and financial purposes control was then transferred to Ford-USA in the early 1990s.

Approval for the XJ-S Facelift

Ford managers arrived at Browns Lane and Whitley within days, and according to insiders one of the very first decisions they made was that the XJ-S facelift should go ahead. The Geoff Lawson team's style was accepted without change, press tools were approved forthwith, and there was every hope that the new-style car would go on the market in the first half of 1991.

Much of the pressure for a revised XJ-S came from the USA where, although the existing car was swelling as never before, the customers were showing every sign of getting bored with the same looks. Not only that, but Mercedes-Benz had just introduced the new-generation SL models, a range of cars that was in direct competition to the XJ-S. 'The restyled car was well overdue,' Mike Cook told me, 'and the styling work was all done even before Ford took over – Ford just guaranteed the funds. In the USA, at the end of 1988/early 1989, we had already looked at what was coming.'

If the reshaped XJS of 1991 was the first visible sign of Ford-approved change at Jaguar, it was by no means the only one, for there were upheavals in management and in what the Americans succinctly call 'real estate'.

Changes in top management saw John Egan leave the company in mid-1990 (to take up the running of the British Airports Authority), to be replaced by a formidable Ford man, Bill Hayden. By 1991, too, technical director Jim Randle had also left the company (he would eventually become a university professor), to be replaced by Clive Ennos from Ford.

Over in North America, Graham Whitehead finally bowed out of Jaguar, bringing his fifty-year involvement with the British motor car industry to a close: although outsiders expected Ford to nominate their own man to run the North American arm, they did not do so, appointing Whitehead's longtime associate Mike Dale instead. In a way, though, Whitehead left a monument behind him in North America, as the brand-new corporate HQ that he had approved was finally opened in 1990:

We had moved from Manhattan to Leonia in 1968, sharing a building with the other British Leyland marques, but our lease was nearly up and we looked round for something new.

We thought we needed a more prestigious HQ, because the product was now completely acceptable, and we were selling more and more cars every year. Incidentally, BMW and Mercedes-Benz had similar styles of HQ ...

A new side window profile was chosen for the facelifted XJS, launched in 1991.

Jaguar XJS V12 5.3-Litre (1991–93)

Layout
Unit-construction steel body/chassis structure. Four-seater, front engine/rear drive, sold as two-door closed coupé or convertible. Style modified from original by different side window profile, and different shape rear lights.

Engine
Type	Jaguar V12
Block material	Cast aluminium
Head material	Cast aluminium
Cylinders	12 in 60-degree vee
Cooling	Water
Bore and stroke	90×70mm
Capacity	5,343cc
Main bearings	7
Valves	2 per cylinder, operated by single-overhead camshaft per cylinder heads, and inverted bucket-type tappets
Compression ratio	12.5:1
Fuel supply	Bosch-Lucas fuel injection
Without catalyst:	
Max. power	290bhp (DIN) @ 5,750rpm
Max. torque	309lb.ft @ 3,150rpm
With catalyst:	
Max. power	284bhp (DIN) @ 5,550rpm
Max. torque	306lb.ft @ 2,800rpm

Transmission
Manual gearbox not available. Automatic transmission (GM400 type) standard.

Internal ratios
Direct	1.00:1
Intermediate	1.48:1
Low	2.48:1
Reverse	2.09:1
Maximum torque multiplication	2.00:1
Final drive ratio	2.88:1

Suspension and steering
Front	Independent, coil springs, wishbones, anti-roll bar, telescopic dampers
Rear	Independent, double coil springs, fixed length drive shafts, lower wishbones, radius arms, twin telescopic dampers
Steering	Rack-and-pinion, power-assisted
Tyres	235/60VR-15in, radial ply
Wheels	Cast aluminium disc, bolt-on
Rim width	6.5in

Brakes

Type	Disc brakes at front and rear, with vacuum servo assistance
Size	11.8in. diameter front, 10.40in diameter rear

Dimensions (in/mm)

Track	
Front	58/1,473
Rear	58.3/1,481
Wheelbase	102/2,591
Overall length	187.5/4,765
Overall width	70.6/1,793
Overall height	50.0/1,270
Unladen weight	Coupé 4,024lb/1,825kg
	Convertible 4,234lb/1,920kg

The glossy new building, at Mahwah, New Jersey (about 30 miles from downtown Manhattan) was officially opened with great pomp and ceremony by Prince Andrew and the Duchess of York.

Not only were Jaguar Cars Inc. therefore ready to receive the restyled XJS, but Jaguar had made new arrangements to build the body shells. Previously, many pressings had been supplied by the Rover Group's pressings plant (ex-Pressed Steel Fisher, of course), but in the late 1980s John Egan set up a new joint project, Venture Pressings Ltd.

Conceived in the late 1980s when Jaguar – and Egan – were in expansionary mode, the new Telford-based pressings plant (west of Wolverhampton) was jointly owned by Jaguar and GKN, the initial strategy being that it would eventually come to supply all future Jaguar pressings to Castle Bromwich. Although it began with new-style XJS pressings at the end of 1990, this enterprise, in fact, would be short-lived, as Ford began rationalize and integrate Jaguar supplies into their own operations for the mid-1990s.

NEW STYLE – A MAJOR FACELIFT

The much revised XJS – note that, officially, the hyphen in the 'XJ-S' title had been abandoned, though this was merely an exercise in semantics that went unnoticed at the time – was introduced in April 1991. Jaguar tacitly acknowledged that this would be the last major change for this long-running car, but would make no comment about the shape, form, or scheduling of its successor. This, then, was the start of The Long Goodbye – which would last until 1996.

The new car was much more than a facelift of the original. Underpinned by Ford finance, not only had Jaguar provided an important restyle, but the six-cylinder engine had been enlarged from 3.6 to 4 litres, both engines would eventually be available with closed or convertible bodywork, and there had also been more development work on suspension and chassis settings.

Visually, the most obvious changes were grouped around the cabin and the tail. From the nose to the screen/front pillar area there seemed to be no important changes, but aft of that there were new

No mistaking the model! Note: XJS, not XJ-S, a change ushered in with the facelift of 1991.

doors, sills, a new roof, boot, rear wings and associated pressings.

Behind the doors there was a new and more rounded side quarter window profile (but if you looked carefully at the rear quarters you could see that these changes were only skin deep), and the boot and rear wings were reshaped, also in a more rounded way, to match a simple new tail lamp cluster that had a horizontal motif and replaced the larger and less graceful style of the original. (Incidentally, when the time came to restyle the XJ6 saloon in 1994, its horizontal rear lamp motif was replaced by a triangular assembly that reminded people of the XJ-S. No consistency there...)

As before, most observers thought (and wrote) that the convertible was still the better-looking of the two new types. Probably this was because the pressed flying buttresses/sail panels linking the roof to the tail had been retained. When questioned, Jaguar insisted that this feature was still positive to the car's image.

Soon after the 1991 XJS was introduced, I asked stylist Colin Holtum about these still-controversial features. He reminded me that coupés without buttresses had indeed been built and had been shown to a selection of typical Jaguar owners in carefully controlled 'clinic' conditions, but that:

> the public told us they preferred the coupé to have its buttresses, so we retained them on the latest car. Without them – well, it just didn't look like an XJ-S, somehow.

When the car was launched to the press, Jim Randle confirmed this opinion, saying that in Jaguar's opinion, a simpler style just 'didn't work'.

On the new-for-1991 model, changes had not only been made to alter the style, but the way it was built, so that it could be made

For the re-style of 1991, Jaguar chose to use simpler tail lamps with a horizontal emphasis, this meaning that new rear wing pressings were also needed. At the same time, officially, XJ-S became XJS, this being signalled by the new style of badges.

better, more quickly, and with more consistent high quality. Although the platform/floorpan was not affected, Jaguar claimed that no fewer than 180 of the 490 pressed panels were either newly styled or modifications of the old. For the first time, all critical body panels were zinc-coated, zinc-phosphated and cathode electrocoated before they were painted: it was this attention to detail that helped spend £4 million at Castle Bromwich, and where Ford expertise helped start the transformation of what had been a small company.

On the new model, not only were there fewer, larger, pressings than before, but all the old-style lead loading that had previously been used to smooth out joints and profiles had been discarded. All in all, this was a more modern way to build what was really an old car, which explains why it was easy to miss the fact that the new car had direct-glazed front and rear glass, new headlamps, doors with frameless window glass and larger diameter road wheels.

Inside the cabin, there was a completely new instrument panel and switchgear layout, for the instrument layout had finally ditched the barrel-type minor dials of the earlier type in favour of analogue dials, and Ford had furnished the latest steering column. There was yet another new style of

Jaguar XJS 4.0-Litre (1991–96)

Layout
Unit-construction steel body/chassis structure. Front engine/rear drive, sold as two-door four-seater coupé from 1991–96, two-seater convertible from 1992–96.

Engine

Type	Jaguar AJ6, in-line six-cylinder
Block material	Cast aluminium
Head material	Cast aluminium
Cylinders	6, in-line
Cooling	Water
Bore and stroke	91×102mm
Capacity	3,980cc
Main bearings	7
Valves	4 per cylinder, operated by twin-overhead camshaft cylinder head, with inverted bucket-type tappets
Compression ratio	9.5:1
Fuel supply	Bosch-Lucas fuel injection
To summer 1994	
Max. power	223bhp (DIN) @ 4,750rpm (USA: 219bhp @ 4,750rpm)
Max. torque	277lb.ft @ 3,650rpm (USA: 273lb.ft @ 3,650rpm)
From summer 1994 with AJ16-type engine	
Max. power	241bhp (DIN) @ 4,700rpm (USA: 237bhp @ 4,700rpm)
Max. torque	282lb.ft @ 4,000rpm (USA: 282lb.ft @ 4,000rpm)

Transmission
Choice of manual or automatic transmissions.
Manual transmission: five-speed all-synchromesh Getrag gearbox.

Internal	
Top	0.76:1
4th	1.00:1
3rd	1.39:1
2nd	2.06:1
1st	3.57:1
Reverse	3.46:1
Final drive ratio	3.54:1

Automatic transmission: four-speed ZF transmission, with torque converter.

Internal ratios

4th	0.73:1
3rd	1.00:1
2nd	1.48:1
1st	2.48:1
Reverse	2.09:1
Maximum torque multiplication	2.00:1
Final drive ratio	3.54:1

Suspension and steering

Front	Independent, coil springs, wishbones, anti-roll bar, telescopic dampers
Rear	Independent, double coil springs, fixed length drive shafts, lower wishbones, radius arms, twin telescopic dampers
Steering	Rack-and-pinion, power-assisted
Tyres	235/60VR-15in, radial-ply
Wheels	Cast aluminium disc, bolt-on
Rim width	6.5in

Brakes

Type	Disc brakes at front and rear, with vacuum servo assistance
Size	11.8in diameter front, 10.40in diameter rear

Dimensions (in/mm)

Track	
Front	58.3/1,481
Rear	58.9/1,495
Wheelbase	102/2,591
Overall length	186.8/4,745
Overall width	70.6/1,793
Overall height	50.0/1,270
Unladen weight	Coupé 3,583lb/1,625kg
	Convertible 3,715lb/1,685kg

The facelift XJS of 1991 incorporated a smart, traditionally styled, facia / instrument panel. After sixteen years with drum-type auxiliary instruments, more traditional round dials were finally chosen. This was the V12 Convertible, complete with airbag in the steering wheel.

steering wheel and column stalks, new electronic-memory seat positions, better rear seats, a new trip computer and better air conditioning. Jaguar claimed that this provided an entirely up-to-date driving environment.

Mechanically, the big news was that the AJ6 engine had been enlarged to 4 litres (by using a longer stroke), which did nothing for peak power, which was actually lower than it had been when introduced in 1983 – catalytic converters and ever-tightening exhaust emission regulations have a lot to answer for! Peak torque, on the other hand, was much higher, at 277lb/ft at 3,650rpm, which made the car much faster in the mid-range and matched the engine better to automatic transmissions.

To match this engine there was the more robust ZF 4HP24 automatic transmission, or the latest Getrag Type 290 five-speed manual gearbox.

By comparison, the V12 engine was merely retouched, with new Lucas fuelling control systems and related electronic controls, a tidier under-bonnet layout of manifolding, wiring and piping, and a minor improvement in peak power, which was back up to 280bhp. This, in fact, was no better than when the car was launched in 1975, but Jaguar, like all other European car-makers, were fighting a continuous (and losing!) battle against regulations, the onset of lower-octane lead-free fuel and stiffer exhaust noise testing.

By any standards, however, this had been a serious programme of rework. The cost of changing any series-production model, especially one where the majority of sales would go to the USA, was spelt out when Jaguar claimed that this facelift had cost £50 million to carry out – the sort of money that simply could not have been afforded without Ford's backing.

The new range went on sale in the UK in May 1991, when the line-up looked like this:

XJS 4-litre Coupé (manual)	£33,400
XJS 4-litre Coupé (auto)	£34,780
XJS 5.3-litre Coupé	£43,500
XJS 5.3-litre Convertible	£50,600

Naturally there was no manual-transmission V12 type, nor would a six-cylinder engined convertible be ready until 1992.

The new-style XJS arrived only just in time, for a world-wide recession had been hitting Jaguar's sales very hard in the early 1990s. XJ-S production, having peaked at 11,207 in 1989, slipped to 9,226 in 1990 then in the year that the latest car was launched it plunged to a mere 4,649.

At first glance this might seem to be because the public did not like the latest car, but the slump was actually caused by a general down-turn in Jaguar sales, particularly in North America. Although Jaguar recovered their position as the 1990s wore on, XJS sales, in fact, would never reach their earlier levels.

To keep the car alive in the next few years Jaguar, urged along by Ford, who were past masters at the art of 'product planning' (that is, the constant refining, changing and fine-tuning of a range) then announced a series of minor changes to keep up the interest, which are best treated chronologically.

Running Changes

May 1992
The 4-litre convertible was finally announced, bringing the XJS range up to four distinct sub-derivatives – two six-cylinder and two V12 types. Unlike the coupé, the 4-litre convertible was only available with automatic transmission, and its early retail UK price was £39,900.

At the same time a driver's side airbag, mounted in the steering wheel hub, became optional (it cost £700 in the UK), and extra stainless-steel X-frame bracing members were added under the front half of the convertible body shell (under the engine/transmission). Amazingly enough, this simple frame was claimed to provide 25 per cent extra torsional rigidity.

September 1992

Manual transmission finally became available on the 4-litre convertible, both convertibles got rear under-floor stiffening struts to add yet more torsional rigidity, and a driver's side airbag was made standard. For

1993 UK-market prices spanned £32,544 (4-litre manual coupé) to £48,864 (5.3-litre V12 convertible).

For the very first time, a six-cylinder XJS model was to be available in the USA, the 4-litre going on sale at $49,750 (coupé) and $56,750 (convertible). Both cars had the full 223bhp, but were only available with automatic transmission at first – the manual transmission version being offered from February 1993. Once offered, the 4-litre version soon began to outsell the V12-engined version, and by 1994 the 4-litre convertible

The 4.0-litre AJ6 six-cylinder engine fitted neatly into Jaguar engine bays, this somehow looking to be a much tidier installation than any V12.

The 6.0-litre V12 engine was finally fitted to mainstream XJS types from 1993, those cars being identified by yet another style of cast alloy road wheels.

would take up three-quarters of all sales. Does this mean that Jaguar should have launched the 'six' years earlier than they did?

May 1993

Until then, every production-line V12-engined XJ-S and XJS had been a 5.3-litre model, but from this point the long-stroke 308bhp 6-litre engine took over instead. Complete with a four-speed GM4L80-E automatic transmission and lower rear axle ratio, outboard rear disc brakes (another Jaguar innovation) and extra 'plus 2' seating in the convertible, this was a substantial change – substantial improvement, many said – on the earlier car.

With 308bhp and a forged crankshaft, the latest engine helped produce a claimed top speed of no less than 161mph (259km/h), making this the fastest V12-engined Jaguar so far. Yet more suspension development had been done, there was new-type ZF power-assisted steering, and there was a new style of six-spoke light alloy road wheel, though you could still get the old-style lattice variety if you asked nicely.

For many, though, it was the arrival of the 2+2 seating that made the most difference. Jaguar explained why this feature could not have been offered from the start of convertible production in 1988 by pointing to the extra engineering, pressing and packaging work involved. Not only were new and extra pressings necessary to form a rear seat pan, but changes also had to be made to the soft top itself.

140

All the latest models were available in the USA by August 1993, so they really counted as 'early 1994' rather than 'late 1993' cars (or 1993½, as the Americans quaintly called them) – except that further changes and improvements went into production at Browns Lane in September 1993, including the fitment of a front passenger airbag as standard, along with major changes to the air-conditioning system!

June 1994

Less than two years before the last XJS of all was built, Jaguar made one final, and very significant, change to the 4-litre car's specification, replacing the original-type AJ6 engine with the much-revised AJ16 variety. This may sound unnecessary, but since the more powerful AJ16 had been developed for the facelifted 'X300' XJ6 saloon, which was due for launch in the autumn of 1994, it actually made good sense to make it standard it in the XJS too.

Although AJ16 was basically the same engine as AJ6, a handsome straight-six, with twin overhead camshafts and four-valves per cylinder, it had new and stiffer cylinder block and head castings, new camshaft profiles,

6.0-litre-engined XJS cars were introduced in 1993, coming with this style of road wheels and with the rationalized type of bonnet pressing. Note the discreet V12 badge on the front wing, behind the wheelarch cut-out.

Jaguar XJS V12 6.0-Litre (1993–95)

Layout

Unit-construction steel body/chassis structure. Four-seater, front engine/rear drive, sold as two-door closed coupé or convertible. Style as for 1991–93 variety.

Engine

Type	Jaguar V12
Block material	Cast aluminium
Head material	Cast aluminium
Cylinders	12 in 60-degree vee
Cooling	Water
Bore and stroke	90 × 78.5mm
Capacity	5,994cc
Main bearings	7
Valves	2 per cylinder, operated by single-overhead camshaft per cylinder heads, and inverted bucket-type tappets
Compression ratio	11.0:1
Fuel supply	Bosch-Lucas fuel injection
Max. power	308bhp (DIN) @ 5,350rpm
Max. torque	355lb.ft @ 2,850rpm

Transmission

Manual gearbox not available. Automatic transmission (GM4L80-E type) standard.

Internal ratios

Fourth	0.75:1
Third	1.00:1
Second	1.48:1
Low	2.48:1
Reverse	2.08:1
Maximum torque multiplication	2.00:1
Final drive ratio	2.88:1

Suspension and steering

Front	Independent, coil springs, wishbones, anti-roll bar, telescopic dampers
Rear	Independent, double coil springs, fixed length drive shafts, lower wishbones, radius arms, twin telescopic dampers
Steering	Rack-and-pinion, power-assisted
Tyres	225/60VR-16in, radial ply
Wheels	Cast aluminium disc, bolt-on
Rim width	7.0in

Brakes

Type	Disc brakes at front and rear, with vacuum servo assistance

Size	11.8in diameter front, 11.60in diameter rear
Dimensions (in/mm)	
Track	
Front	58/1,473
Rear	58.3/1,481
Wheelbase	102/2,591
Overall length	187.5/4,765
Overall width	70.6/1,793
Overall height	50.0/1,270
Unladen weight	Coupé 4,101lb/1,860kg
	Convertible 4,377lb/1,985kg

The XJS airbag system, as installed in the hub of the steering wheel. Such bags were only ever intended to be used in conjunction with safety belts, not instead of them.

Browns Lane 1994, and several generations of Jaguar posing outside the administrative offices. An XJS is parked alongside a late-1940s Mark V and a latest-generation XJ6, with an SS100 sports car in the background.

and further developed fuel injection, electronics and engine management systems.

Although even more refined, quieter and with a 'cleaner' exhaust system than before, it was also more powerful and more torquey. Considering that the engine design team was already working away on a new V8 design for XK8 (*see* Chapter 8), it was amazing that so much could be, and had been, done.

Here is a comparison between AJ6 and AJ16:

	Peak Power @ RPM	Peak Torque @ RPM
AJ6 4-litre	223bhp/4,750	277lb.ft/3,650
AJ16 4-litre	241bhp/4,700	282lb.ft/4,000

As far as Jaguar customers were concerned, this was almost power for free, for there was 18bhp (or 8 per cent) more peak power than before, and a little more torque. For the XJS, the top speed claim had risen to 147mph (237km/h), with 0–60 being achieved in 6.9 seconds. At the same time a new trim/furnishing package was introduced, and the bumper colour-keying (matching colours to the body colour) that had been applied to the bumpers in 1993, was also extended to the grille, headlamp surrounds and the door mirrors.

From mid-1994 the UK prices line-up was:

4-litre Coupé (manual)	£36,800
4-litre Coupé (auto)	£38,250

4-litre Convertible (manual)	£45,100
4-litre Convertible (auto)	£46,550
5.3-litre Coupé	£50,500
5.3-litre Convertible	£58,800

In nearly two decades, therefore, British inflation and a continual push up-market had done terrible things to price levels. In 1975 the original V12-engined XJ-S Coupé had cost £8,900 – and now it was £50,500 – a 567 per cent rise.

Although the XJS was something of an automotive dinosaur by this time, it had also been developed into a formidable machine, which independent road testers continued to love. Having got rid of their ritual jibes about the size, the looks and the weight, most invariably returned to the fact that here was an impressively refined machine, effortless to drive, with a magnificent combination of roadholding, ride and refinement that every other competitor in the world was anxious to match – and could not.

Autocar's Stephen Sutcliffe drove an AJ16-equipped car in July 1994, commenting that:

> More importantly, they also transform the gritty, slightly strained nature of the ancient AJ6 into something altogether more polished – and that's not Jaguar hype, it's real …
>
> … the XJS is a good deal more refined with the AJ16 [engine]. Put your foot down and although that delicious straight six Jaguar bark is still there, lift off and it tapers away to a distant hum that is more relaxing yet more cultured than before. No question at all: this is one slick drivetrain.

When the same magazine compared the 4-litre with a BMW 840, the test driver concluded:

> The Jaguar savours its performance as a refined, standard-English-tool for conveying its pomp and luxury across great distance …

This was the final version of the XJS Convertible, complete with the restyled tail, and with a 4.0-litre 6-cylinder engine under the bonnet.

I mean, sitting in the XJS surrounded by warm colours, textures and smells feels like my Dad's reading den – not the most clever place in the world, but I want to be there. Does anyone do leather, chrome and wood this well? Cabin space is painfully restricted, though, with a sense of confinement that is not helped by restricted 'four panel' front seats.

One of my colleagues came up with a brilliant line about how a Rolls-Royce dignifies the journey, not the occupants. That's how I feel about the Jaguar, really. It has a wonderful ride, a gloriously revived engine and a cabin that makes even minor trips an occasion. It will make you feel better about yourself, I promise.

This, therefore, was at once the high point of the XJS's career, and the beginning of its end. For the rest of its career, the important dates commemorate endings, not beginnings.

May 1995

To mark their sixtieth anniversary, Jaguar chose to sell a short series of 'Celebration' cars, which were mechanically little changed, but had extra trim and furnishing touches such as leather seat facings, and yet another style of road wheel, this being the Aerosport 7 × 16in cast alloys.

Regular production of V12-engined cars ceased at this time (but continued to special order for a few more months), one reason being that the 4-litre car had almost completely taken over from the V12 car in North America. In 1995, in fact, only 413 V12-engined XJS cars were sold in the USA – a mere 10 per cent of 4-litre sales. The last V12-engined car of all, in fact, was built in the first few days of 1996.

March 1996

After months of rumour, Jaguar confirmed that the XJS was near the end of its career, by previewing a new-generation car, the

Two views of the 1996-model 'Celebration' 4.0-litre models, showing off the final tail-end style, and the special XJR-S style wheels.

This is probably the most flattering view of all for the XJS Convertible, showing the surprisingly confined cockpit for such a large car. This was the 1996 'Celebration' 4-litre model.

V8-engined XK8, of which a coupé version was displayed at the Geneva Motor Show. A few weeks later the XK8 Convertible was shown at the New York Show.

In many ways the new XK8 was based on the chassis/platform of the old XJS, and I have analysed these links, and the new car, in the next chapter.

April 1996

Somewhat earlier than expected, the last XJSs of all – a coupé and a convertible – were built at Browns Lane on 4 April 1996. These final examples were both acquired by the Jaguar Daimler Heritage Trust Collection and were meant to be used in displays and demonstrations in the years to come.

Because Jaguar dealers still had some XJS types in stock, and because of the obvious 'pipeline effect' of cars being shipped to export markets, Jaguar expected to have cars to sell until the very first XK8s were delivered later in the year.

A placard fixed to the top of the last cars for publicity purposes, said this:

THE LAST OF THE SERIES
XJS – 1975 to 1996

CONVERTIBLE CARS BUILT	30,946
CABRIOLET CARS BUILT	5,013
COUPÉ CARS BUILT	79,454
TOTAL CARS BUILT	115,413

A sad, yet a proud occasion at Browns Lane in April 1996, when the last two XJ-S cars of all were completed. This was the final convertible, a red car …

… this being the last car of all, a blue coupé. In 1996, Jaguar claimed to have built 115,413 cars, but later a recount put the figure at 115,330.

Jaguar production 1975–96 and XJ-S production

Year	Total production	XJ-S production	Comment on XJ-S events
1975	24,295	1,245	XJ-S first put on sale
1976	31,903	3,082	
1977	23,688	3,890	
1978	27,346	3,121	
1979	14,861	2,405	
1980	15,262	1,057	XJ-S production suspended for some months following poor USA sales
1981	13,812	1,292	Introduction of new HE model
1982	21,934	3,478	First XJ-S victories in European Touring Car Championship
1983	27,331	4,749	Introduction of XJ-S Cabriolet, and of new-generation AJ6 6-cylinder engine
1984	33,355	6,509	Jaguar company privatized
1985	38,500	7,951	Introduction of Cabriolet V12
1986	41,437	9,052	
1987	48,020	9,826	
1988	51,939	10,356	Introduction of Convertible: Cabriolet discontinued. JaguarSport XJR-S announced
1989	48,139	11,207	Jaguar taken over by Ford. Record year for XJ-S production
1990	41,833	9,226	
1991	23,018	4,649	Serious sales slump due to British recession Restyled XJ-S introduced
1992	22,474	3,633	
1993	27,338	5,192	V12 engine enlarged to 6.0-litre in XJS. Aston Martin DB7 previewed, using a modified XJS floorpan
1994	30,020	6,918	AJ16 6-cylinder engine replaces AJ6 engine type. Aston Martin DB7 deliveries begin
1995	41,042	4,884	
1996	38,588	1,608	Final XJS produced in April, New V8-engined XK8 previewed in March, with sales beginning in the autumn

Total XJ-S production, 1975 to 1996, was 115,330

Details:	XJ-S with manual gearbox	352 cars produced
	XJ-S Cabriolet production	1,150 3.6-litre cars 3,863 5.3-litre V12 cars
	XJR-S (TWR) production	300 5.3-litre cars approx. 500 6.0-litre cars approx.

The last two XJSs of all bracket one of the very first V8-engined XK8s, in the assembly hall at Browns Lane in April 1996. The XK8, in fact, was to be built on developed versions of the long-evolved XJS platform.

	XJ-S sales in the USA: 1975 to 1996				
Year	**Coupé V12**	**Cabriolet V12**	**Convertible V12**	**Coupé 4.0-litre 6-cylinder**	**Convertible 4.0-litre 6-cylinder**
1975	287				
1976	1,365				
1977	869				
1978	1,050				
1979	695				
1980	420				
1981	232				
1982	1,409				
1983	2,705				
1984	3,480				
1985	3,784				
1986*	4,286	575			
1987	3,527	1,015	838**		
1988	2,448	321	2,014***		
1989	1,901	1	2,556		
1990	1,658		3,057		
1991	1,008		1,730		
1992	702		1,356		
1993	139		348	613	1,866
1994	109		632	388	3,163
1995	51		362	364	3,758
1996	1		26	2	2,113

*   Also 24 3.6-litre 6-cylinder cars, details unspecified
**   All Hess & Eisenhardt conversions, USA produced, from coupés
*** Approximately 1,000 of these were Hess & Eisenhardt conversions, the balance being factory-produced cars.

The final XJS facia / instrument panel, complete with round-dial instruments, an airbag steering wheel and an airbag ahead of the passenger, was very different from the original 1975–81 variety.

In the end, therefore, the XJS had confounded all its critics and returned its investment to the company. Praised for its performance, handling, ride and refinement, it had originally been slammed for its heavy fuel consumption and its looks, but Jaguar never lost faith.

Even though the XJS sold so slowly in the early years, and the build quality had often been poor, Jaguar persisted with it, improved it, widened the range, and in particular turned it into the archetypal British Grand Tourer.

In modern times, the world of motoring has often seen the arrival of cars that have been lavishly praised, but that have nevertheless been commercial failures. It has also seen new models smeared by the press, but persistently bought by the clientele. In most cases such cars are full of character, and certainly cannot be ignored. The XJS was one of those cars, and brushed off all criticism.

In many ways, therefore, the XJS was an ugly duckling that gradually turned into a swan. Those who say that it was no substitute for the E-Type should remember two basic statistics – it outsold the E-Type by no fewer than 43,000 cars, and had a much longer production life. By any standards, this had been a remarkable career.

8 The New Generation – XK8 Meets Its Public

Can you believe that this car – the Jaguar XK8 – is based on the same platform as the XJS?

Even before the last XJS was built, its successor – to be badged XK8 – had already been previewed. In a carefully calculated attempt to raise the public's interest before deliveries could possibly begin, Jaguar showed prototypes of the new car, yet held back many details of their specification. The public got its first sight of the XK8 Coupé at Geneva in March 1996, and of the convertible in New York in April.

XJ41 – AN INTRIGUING FALSE START

This was not the first time that Jaguar had considered replacing the XJS. Project work actually began in the mid-1980s, and by the time the design and development departments moved from Browns Lane to Whitley, much of their time was taken up with work on new projects carrying the code XJ41.

Although this was naturally a secret project, some news and a number of spy pictures leaked out. Even before Ford took over Jaguar at the end of 1989, speculation had begun about a car that the press dubbed a new 'F-Type'. This, it was said, would be launched before the end of 1990, would be powered by developments of the modern 24-valve six-cylinder engine, and would be available with rear-wheel-drive or four-wheel-drive.

Speculations on the style suggested shapes that later influenced the Aston Martin DB7 (*see* the panel on page 156), but when challenged, Jaguar would only confirm that 'work is progressing on a sports car project for the 1990s', and left it at that.

Several prototypes had been built by the end of 1989, but by this time the projected launch date had slipped by several years. By this time the latest 4-litre version of the 24-valve AJ6 – in normally aspirated or twin-turbocharged form – had come into use. The four-wheel-drive system was being finalized by FF Developments, the successor to Harry Ferguson Research, and whose 4 × 4 credentials spanned cars as different as the original Jaguar XJ220 show car, the Jensen FF of the late 1960s, and Ford's beautiful RS200 Group B rally car of the mid-1980s.

Somewhere along the way, though, the project had gone awry, gaining weight at every change and development, and rising rapidly in costs. Only months after Jaguar had taken control, the project was cancelled, the prototypes being stored away. When I began the writing of a book about Jaguar XJ models (*Jaguar XJ Series – the Complete Story*, published by The Crowood Press) I actually spent time talking to Jaguar stylists in the studios at Whitley, with shrouded, cancelled, XJ41 prototypes only a few yards away!

One reason for cancellation was that weights and costs had both risen alarmingly,

but another was that the styling, which had been settled in 1988, would not have looked sufficiently fresh by 1993 or 1994 when it could finally have been put on sale. Interviewed just before he stepped down from Jaguar (and before joining BAA plc), Sir John Egan conceded that the XJ41 had been overweight and underpowered, 'but it was also very beautiful'. Bill Hayden, the brutally blunt-spoken ex-Ford man who replaced Sir John as Jaguar's chairman, confirmed this:

> The XJ41 failed to meet one single performance objective; it was grossly, hundreds of pounds, overweight. We could have kept slogging it out, but in the long run it seemed better to cut our losses.

From that moment on, there was never any question of the XJ41 being revived, or even given a stay of execution. The whole idea of new-generation sports cars was abandoned for the time being, for Jaguar then turned to developing the much-revised XJ6 models, which finally went on sale in 1994.

X100 – AN IMPRESSIVE NEW PROGRAMME

Once cancelled, the XJ41 programme was speedily consigned to history – yet Jaguar would not reveal picture or even sketches of that car. The whole idea was blocked out of their thinking, their heritage, as if it had never been. In particular, the 4 × 4 transmission philosophy was abandoned.

With Whitley's design and development team totally committed to X300 (new generation XJ6 work), plans for an XJ-S replacement went into limbo. Except for the design of a totally new generation V8 engine by Trevor Crisp's team – a 'building block' that was intended for use in several future Jaguars, little work was done.

Before the end of 1991, however, a window of opportunity began to open up. X300 work had been completed, and work on the exciting new 'small Jaguar' (to be revealed before the end of the 1990s) had not gone far. Working to a brief that a completely new body style could be worked up around the existing XJS platform, some of the inner structure and the suspensions, Geoff Lawson's styling team started work on a new 2+2 model – X100.

Serious work began in January 1992 (less than a year after the fully facelifted XJS had gone on sale), always on the basis of a car using the XJS's wheelbase, and slightly modified versions of the wheel tracks. Those

were the 'given' features, the major novelties being a brand new and curvaceous body style, a new five-speed ZF automatic transmission – and a brand-new V8 engine, coded the AJ-V8.

Within months several full-size clay models had been worked up, selected 'target' customers on both sides of the Atlantic were brought in to view the results, and by mid-summer 1992 a coupé close to the final style had evolved. At this stage, please note, no convertible (not even a lath-and-plaster mock-up) had been produced.

Final approval for the definitive X100 (the new car was still a long way from having its final title – XK8 – chosen) came in

Although the XJ8 of 1996 was based on the platform of the XJS, the superstructure was entirely different, as was the new-generation V8 engine.

Based on the XJS's platform, the XK8 looked completely different – although it had the same wheelbase and similar tracks and suspensions.

October 1992, after which prototype construction, testing and gruelling long-term development began. Visually there was no comparison between the XJS and X100 – the new car being considerably more rounded, with a slightly shorter nose and bonnet (the use of a squat V8 engine instead of the long AJ16 or bulky V12 units helped a lot here) – for even the five-spoke alloy wheels were new. Compared with the XJS, though, the cabin was larger, for the screen was further forward than before and the rear window further back.

While Jaguar and Aston Martin admitted that the XJS formed the structural basis of

the XK8 and the DB7, both insist that there was no question of the cars sharing the same body skin panels. Mechanically, too, they were widely different, not only because the Aston Martin used a specially developed version of the straight-six cylinder 3.2-litre AJ16, but because of totally different transmissions (including a manual transmission option), and alloy wheels. [Even so, when I walked into Jaguar North America's New Jersey HQ in March 1996, ahead of the release of the XK8 Convertible at the New York Show, and saw a DB7 standing in the foyer, it made me pause for a moment.]

Aston Martin DB7 – How much XJS under the skin?

This is not something that Aston Martin or Jaguar is happy to talk about – at least in detail. If you looked carefully under the skin of the Aston Martin DB7, which went on sale during 1994, you would find an amazing amount of familiar Jaguar XJS hardware – not just the bare bones of the engine, but the transmission, the suspension, and the modified platform too.

In fact this is a simple little story, the connection of course being Ford. Ford took control of Aston Martin at the end of 1987, and of Jaguar in 1989, and it was soon obvious that a degree of rationalization might be appropriate. Soon after Ford appointed its distinguished elder statesman, Walter Hayes, to be Aston Martin's Chairman, work on a new Aston Martin model began in earnest.

Time to step back a pace. As already detailed in the main text, Jaguar had spent time in the 1980s designing and developing the XJ41 sports coupé, whose aim in life was to take over from the XJS. The XJ41, however, was cancelled soon after Ford took control, the prototypes being banished, to sit under dust sheets in Jaguar's design centre at Whitley.

In the meantime Walter Hayes set up Aston Martin Oxford with Tom Walkinshaw's TWR Group, and work was started on a Jaguar-based 'XX' car in 1991. The Aston Martin NPX (Newport Pagnell Experimental) followed in 1992. From the beginning, the plan was for Aston Martin Oxford to engineer the car, and for it to be produced at the JaguarSport Bloxham factory (near Banbury), just as soon as assembly of Jaguar XJ220s had ceased.

Prototypes of the DB7, in fact, were unveiled in March 1993, well before deliveries could begin, the first customer cars actually not leaving Bloxham until the summer of 1994, priced at £78,500.

The DB7's fastback coupé style was by Ian Callum of TWR and, to quote Walter Hayes:

> We photographed the most beautiful DB4s and DB6s we could find, stuck the pictures up in the studio, and said 'Like that' ...

– those in the know say that the DB7 looks rather like the cancelled XJ41, which may be true, but in any case it stands on its own as a beautiful machine.

Although Aston Martin insists that the DB7 uses a unique pressed platform, there is no doubt that it uses a modified and updated version of the XJS layout, with identical wheelbase and slightly wider track dimensions. The suspension layouts – most noticeably the independent rear suspension, complete with its massive pressed bridge supporting the axle, springs, dampers and pivots – are clearly Jaguar-derived.

The DB7's engine was a modified version of the Jaguar AJ16 3.2-litre, complete with Eaton supercharger, and produced 335bhp at 5,500rpm. In late 1994 this compared with the 241bhp normally-aspirated Jaguar 3.2-litre in the XJS, and with the 321bhp supercharged 4.0-litre types fitted to the new-generation XJ6 saloons.

Behind the engine there was a choice of Getrag five-speed all-synchromesh, or ZF 4HP22 four-speed automatic transmissions, these also being the transmissions then being used in the six-cylinder engined XJS.

So, what if it was really a Jaguar XJS under a stylish new body? To quote the *Autocar* road test of the DB7 in October 1994:

> It is no coincidence that the DB7 shares engine and suspension designs with the Jaguar XJS. Deep, deep in its history, it *is* an XJS ...

Aston Martin has never commented on the DB7's tortured genesis and nor need it. It only knows how badly it needed NPX, Jag-based or not ...

Haven't fashions changed since the XJS was styled in the early 1970s? This was the original XK8 of 1996, still using the XJS chassis platform, but with a rounded profile, and no sign of separate front or rear bumpers.

THE AJ-V8 ENGINE

Because the XK8's 4-litre V8 engine was brand new, there were no carry-over links with previous XJS power units, though the same team, headed by Trevor Crisp, had also been responsible for the older AJ6/AJ16 six-cylinder types. It is quite amazing to realize that this was only the fourth all-new engine design Jaguar Cars had put into production in fifty years !

The 4-litre AJ-V8 was not only very powerful – at 294bhp, it was almost as powerful as the last of the 6-litre V12s – but it was packed with innovative detail. Not only was it a 32-valve four-cam unit, but it was also equipped with variable inlet camshaft timing, plastic inlet manifolding, and many other subtle improvements over the old type. Light, compact and amazingly torquey, this was clearly an important building block for Jaguar's future.

Incidentally, although the concept and detail design was all Jaguar, manufacture was actually to be based at Ford's Bridgend plant in South Wales. It is also interesting to note that the complex, lightweight, cylinder head and cylinder block castings were being supplied by Cosworth, which had built a new factory in Worcester especially for that purpose.

Purely for interest, how new and old engines stack up is shown in the box opposite.

XK8 STRUCTURE – XJS UNDER THE SKIN

Although details of the XK8's chassis were withheld until the car was ready to go on sale, Jaguar never made a secret of the fact that the basic architecture of the XJS had

been retained. Some pundits made much of the fact that this architecture was old – the XJS, after all, was in production for more than twenty years, and had itself been developed from the underpan of the 1968-style XJ6 – but most ignored just how effective that platform had always been.

In the mid-1990s, as in the mid-1970s, the XJS's ride and refinement levels were unsurpassed (Bob Knight, his passion for quiet and refined cars always well to the fore, had made sure of that), so there was little need for major change to be made for the XK8. However, although the same basic pressed steel platform was carried over from the XJS, considerable changes were made to the suspension layout. At the front, there was a totally new double wishbone system, all mounted on a complex diecast aluminium subframe (which was itself 13lb/6kg lighter

For the XK8 of 1996, the new-generation AJ-V8 4-litre engine took over from two older types – the 4.0-litre AJ16 six-cylinder engine and the 6.0-litre V12.

Comparison of old and new Jaguar engines			
Engine	Capacity (bore × stroke)	Peak power bhp/rpm	Peak torque lb.ft/rpm
AJ-V8	3,996cc (86 × 86mm)	294/6,100	290/4,250
V12 (1993)	5,994cc (90 × 78.5mm)	308/5,350	355/2,850
AJ16 (1994)	3,980cc (91 × 102mm)	241/4,700	282/4,000

No fewer than five generations of Jaguar sportscar are caught in this 1996 display. With the 1996 XK8 in the foreground, other cars (right to left) are the XJS of 1995, a mid-1960s E-Type, the famous ex-Ian Appleyard XK120 rally car of 1950, and a late-1930s SS100.

than the XJS subframe which it replaced), while at the rear, the classic Jaguar layout of fixed-length drive shafts along with transverse lower arms owed a lot more to the latest-generation XJ6/XJR installation.

As with the obsolete XJS, there was not to be any choice of transmission, for all cars were built with automatic transmission, a

ZF five-speeder, of the type already chosen for use in the biggest and best BMWs. This, together with electronic traction control by Teves/ITT (which used the same basic systems as the anti-lock braking sensors), and the very latest 17in rubber from Pirelli, provided an extremely capable, and extremely safe, 155mph (250kph) projectile.

It was still a 2+2-seater, and although almost every tester agreed that it was slightly more roomy than the XJS had ever been, they also agreed that rivals could offer more space. Because the 'chassis' of the XK8 was so obviously derived from that of the XJS, Jaguar's publicity staff trod a very careful line when describing the new car, pointing out that 90 per cent of it was new – yet they need not have worried.

By the time the XK8 went on sale in the UK, in October 1996, stocks of XJS models had virtually been exhausted. It is interesting, even so, to show a very simple 1996 price comparison between the two types:

Last XJS 4-litre 6-cylinder coupé	£38,950
Last XJS 4-litre 6-cylinder convertible	£45,950
First XK8 4-litre V8 coupé	£47,950
First XK8 4-litre V8 convertible	£54,950

Jaguar, in other words, was charging £9,000 more for the new car, complete with its V8 engine. If this was likely to deter anyone from buying the new models, it did not show, for waiting lists were already long when the car went on sale, and a few XK8s with 'delivery mileage' were soon being advertised at prices a lot higher than that!

Time after time, testers wrote ecstatically of the XK8's performance, its style *and* of its impeccable road manners. The superlative performance, I agree, was all to the credit of the all-new V8 engine, and the style was unique, but the road manners, no question, were merely a development of those which the XJS had been providing for so long.

Autocar's testers, who had taken part in pre-production testing in North America, probably summed up everyone's opinion:

The XK8 was worth the wait. Worth those thousands of miles perfecting the ride in America, the sub-zero testing in Lapland, the arguments over it's styling which raged for months anywhere from Cologne to Coventry. It is a truly accomplished GT car … To the outside world, the XK8 is every inch the class act it so richly promises to be …

Yet could it have been achieved without two decades of XJS experience? I doubt it.

9   XJ-S in Motor Racing

At first sight you wouldn't expect the XJ-S to be a good racing car. For a start, how would you categorize it? Was it a touring car, a GT machine, or even a sports car?

There was also the problem of its sheer bulk. By the 1970s the way to win on the circuits was to use the lightest cars with the biggest tyres that could squeeze into the regulations. Although it was very powerful, the XJ-S didn't come out top in any of those categories, for it was big and heavy.

Then there were the politics of the situation – and in the British Leyland era we must never forget the politics! Jaguar had been officially out of motor sport since the 1950s, and by the 1970s British Leyland had closed down all their competitions activities. But that was only for a few years, so that by the mid-1970s there had been a gradual reawakening of interest.

Once British Leyland had been nationalized, the Leyland Cars division (under Derek Whittaker) reopened a competitions department. Ralph Broad's Broadspeed concern started by racing Triumph Dolomite Sprints, but soon persuaded Whittaker that he could do an even better job with Jaguars in 1976 in the European Touring Car Championship.

For no very good reason, Leyland Cars decided that they wanted Broadspeed to use XJ 5.3C four-seaters instead of the new XJ-S, and the result was a two-season farrago of retirements, non-starts and failure to win. Under the existing Appendix J Group 2 regulations, where certain mini-

mum cabin dimensions were specified, there was certainly the problem that the XJ-S was rather tightly dimensioned. Another, according to Jaguar authority Andrew Whyte, was that Jaguar Engineering did not approve. (But, in that case, why did they approve of an XJ5.3C being used instead? The two cars, after all, shared all the same basic running gear, and it can't have been a question of aerodynamics, surely?)

No matter. After two embarrassing years of racing with Broadspeed XJ 5.3Cs sporting huge wheelarch flares and lurid colour schemes, the Jaguar sporting effort was rapidly wound up, and forgotten as soon as decently possible.

WINNING IN THE USA

Over in the USA, however, calmer and more experienced bosses had better ideas. Group 44, a renowned independent racing operation, headed by Bob Tullius, had won many races with Jaguar E-Types, including an SCCA National Championship in 1975 – and of course with a whole variety of Triumphs – and was most anxious to repeat the trick with the new XJ-S.

Because the XJ-S was so much larger – and heavier – than the E-Type SIII that it displaced, this was never going to be easy. Graham Whitehead, President of the Jaguar operation, had always been an enthusiastic supporter of Group 44, and was soon persuaded to back the team in the TransAm series. He recalls:

> There were not many V12s around, and we thought the XJ-S needed a lot of advertising, support and promotion. We did a lot of motor racing with Bob Tullius.
>
> It was an expensive programme, but we thought it was important – we thought that the success did a lot for the ambience of Jaguar in the USA. Although the number of people actually seeing the races was really quite small, we were always ready to advertise successes – often in the newspapers only a day or two later.
>
> At the time it was a vitally important part of our marketing programme.

Based close to Washington, in immaculate quarters, Group 44 set out to prepare a new XJ-S for TransAm racing, this being a completely professional series that was already being supported by domestic manufacturers from Detroit.

Along with his engineer/driver partner Brian Fuerstenau, Tullius's first cars looked conventional enough, though very substantial roll cages were fitted, along with race-spec suspensions, wider wheels, tyres and enlarged brakes.

The first V12 engines used dry-sump layouts, ran with six Weber twin-choke carburettors, and produced a lusty 475bhp at 7,600rpm. Transmission was in the hands of Jaguar's normal four-speed all-synchromesh gearbox, backed by a race-prepared Salisbury-type differential.

Although Tullius's first car could only finish fourth in his first event in 1976, it won outright on its second outing, at Lime Rock. With suitable gearing the Group 44 car could beat 180mph (290km/h), so clearly its potential was enormous.

During 1977, Group 44 made a full assault on the TransAm series, chasing championship points all round the continent in the 500bhp car – in the USA and in Canada. All in all, there were ten races, the longest being a six-hour marathon at Mosport.

This was a typical, assured, Group 44 effort, for Tullius himself won his category five times – half the races, in other words – which was quite enough to secure the Drivers' Championship in his division. The most outstanding performance came at Mosport, where Tullius shared the car with Fuerstenau, winning outright.

There was even more success in 1978, for this was the season in which Group 44 entered two cars – 'Old No. 1' and a brand-new machine. Better, faster, more nimble and more reliable than before, the cars were always competitive. Not only did the XJ-S repeat its six-hour victory (this time at Watkins Glen circuit, in northern New York state), but there were six other category victories, spread as far apart as Montreal (Canada) and Mexico City. Not only did Tullius win the Drivers' Championship again – this was becoming a habit for him, for Jaguar, and for Group 44 – but the XJ-S also won the Manufacturers' Championship as well.

SPACE-FRAME XJ-S FINALE

British Leyland's serious financial problems then led to wholesale cut-backs in marketing expenditure, which meant that Group 44 lost their Jaguar sponsorship, and had to return to racing Triumphs. The result was that the XJ-Ss were put away, and did not compete in the 1979 and 1980 Championship season.

Then, in 1981, Group 44's racing involvement with Jaguar was revived in a sensational manner. John Egan had arrived in Coventry, the sales atmosphere in the USA was improving, and with the XJ-AS HE on the horizon Jaguar thought it was time to start banging the racing drum once again.

When Graham Whitehead made the 'we're back' announcement in March 1981, he made it clear that Group 44 were aiming for outright victories, and that he would not be satisfied with anything less. While the XJ-S had been 'in retirement' the TransAm rules had changed considerably, and it was now possible to build 'silhouette' cars with entirely different structures.

For 1981, therefore, the 'XJ-S' might have looked nearly standard, but most certainly was not. This was a specially designed racing car that just happened to look similar to an XJ-S and used the famous V12 engine!

The standard monocoque shell had been abandoned, and in its place there was a tubular frame (using NASCAR-style technology and build methods), clad by lightweight XJ-S-style skin panels. In that sturdy frame, a 550bhp version of the engine was mounted about 7.5in (190mm) further back than standard, while the suspension was mainly built up from specially designed Group 44 components. In addition, there was a Franckland quick-change differential, though the rear discs remained inboard.

If this represented brute force, it was certainly not ignorance, and Group 44 looked

Daytona 1981, with Group 44 founder/star driver Bob Tullius at the wheel of the formidable XJ-S car. By that time, and still within the regulations, this was not so much a modified XJ-S as a tubular-framed race car which just happened to use a Jaguar V12 engine, and have a body style rather like the XJ-S.

Over the years, the Group 44 XJ-S race cars got wider and wider. By 1981 Bob Tullius's car carried vast wheelarch flares and 'roller-width' tyres – seen here on the banking at Daytona in the 1981 SCCA race.

forward to a very exciting – and competitive – 1981 season. All but two of the nine events were held in the USA, the sixth and seventh rounds being held in Canada.

Although everything did not go according to plan, the tubular-framed 'XJ-S' was always on the pace. Tullius started the season at Charlotte (North Carolina) and finished second, went on to win the next race at Portland, Oregon, then failed to finish the next two races when side-lined by engine electrical problems.

After winning at Brainerd (Minnesota) and finishing second in Quebec, Tullius won once again at Mosport, Ontario, so there was still a real chance of lifting the Championship crowns once again. In Round 8, however, at Laguna Seca (California), the XJ-S had gearbox problems, and could only finish fifth, while in the last round at Sears Point (California) Tullius had to retire with a damaged gearbox seal. Although Tullius had won three races – more than anyone else in the series – it wasn't quite enough for him to win the Championship: the record books show that he finished second overall.

This was almost the end of the XJ-S racing career in North America, for Group 44 and Jaguar Cars Inc. had even more ambitious racing plans that would involve the building of a new mid-engined racing two-seater sports car – the XJR-5.

Even so, this was not quite the end for the XJ-S. Early in 1982 the space-frame car started the Daytona 24-hour race (Tullius's co-drivers were Bill Adam and Gordon Smiley), and although the car was timed at 94.46mph (151.99km/h), the gearbox gave trouble so no creditable results were achieved. Three months later, Gordon Smiley was tragically killed at Indianapolis when trying to qualify an entirely different car for the Indy 500 race, and the project was abandoned. The XJ-S never raced again.

But as one door closed, another was about to open. Even as Group 44 were retiring the XJ-S, back in the UK a determined Scot was starting his own racing programme ...

NEW RULES, NEW OPPORTUNITIES

By the early 1980s Tom Walkinshaw had built a great reputation, not only as a racing driver, but as a businessman, and was already formidably successful in touring car racing. When motor sport's governing body decided to change the regulations, bringing in a new series of categories – Groups N, A, B and C – for 1982, Walkinshaw analysed his opportunities.

As far as Group A and the European Touring Car Championship were concerned, the

Years before the XJ-S started to win races in Europe, it was a dominant car in North American SCCA sports car racing. This was Bob Tullius's Group 44 car at Lime Rock in 1981.

new regulations would make sure the cars *looked* more standard than before, even though there was still to be a large degree of technical freedom. Touring cars would no longer be allowed to use massive wheelarch flares and ultra-wide wheels and tyres, extra 'add-on' aerodynamic features were banned, and there was to be a new sliding scale of minimum weight/engine size limits.

Walkinshaw was a great believer in winning from the front. He saw no merit in trying to win classes, or even trying to scrape home to victory, with cars whose engines were not the most powerful in the field. But he was not interested in using the XJ5.3C –

especially after the shambles that had resulted from the Broadspeed programme.

In fact BL's director of motor sport, John Davenport, had asked him to sit down, scan the BL range, and work out which car in the entire BL range would be best for ETC (European Touring Car) racing – expecting him to confirm the choice of a Rover SD1. Walkinshaw, though, had other ideas in 1981:

I realized first and foremost that the ideal car for the job would have double wishbone suspension [the SD1 had a MacPherson strut], for Group A allows generous wheel

Tom Walkinshaw's TWR team started campaigning XJ-S race cars in 1982, those first cars using 400bhp 5.3-litre V12 engines, which were mated to the old-style four-speed manual transmission. The first victory in the European Touring Championship came in June, at the Czechoslovakian Brno circuit.

166

and tyre widths but no changes to the exterior bodywork.

A car with a wishbone suspension therefore allows you greater unimpeded depth inside the wheelarch.

When I drew up the optimum car, as well as double wishbones, I wanted something with fuel injection. The XJ-S fitted the bill. To be honest, the fact that the XJC did not work worried me. But the more I looked at its history, the more convinced I became that it should have worked ...

In any case, why use a heavy car like the XJ5.3C (which had been out of production since the end of 1977) if a lighter car with the same running gear – the XJ-S – already existed? First of all Walkinshaw had to measure the cabin to see that the XJ-S qualified as a 'four-seater', which indeed it did. And, for those who think this must have been a marginal case, please remember that one of the XJ-S's principal competitors was the BMW 635 Coupé, whose cabin was probably smaller.

Having seen the way that Bob Tullius's XJ-Ss had performed so well in North American motor sport, he wondered whether the same type of car might not be ideal in Europe too? Could an XJ-S be made into a race winner in a series where events would be a minimum of 500km (310miles) or 3½ hours long, where the rules would not allow the wheelarches to be enlarged, or where the Jaguar would have to run at a minimum weight of 1,400kg (3,087lb), with a fuel tank no larger than 120 litres (26.4 Imperial gallons)?

Although Walkinshaw then made his first approach to Jaguar – to chairman John Egan, no less – in 1981, he was not to know that Jaguar's own engineers had already been investigating the XJ-S's potential. Even before the disastrous Broadspeed programme was cancelled, it seemed time had been spent looking at a possible 'Group 5'

project to match what Porsche was doing with the 935, though this would have involved much-modified bodywork, and the use of a large rear spoiler.

When Walkinshaw met Egan, there was good news and bad news. On the one hand, Egan refused to put any money into a proposed TWR programme for 1982, but on the other hand, he offered great encouragement in terms of facilities and technical support, and the promise that if Walkinshaw did well, there would definitely be support for 1983.

In 1982 BL's spokesmen stated:

> We will, of course, be watching the car's progress closely, but we are in no way involved in the same way we were involved in the last Jaguar ETC project.

Jaguar's chairman, John Egan confirmed this attitude when the 1983 programme was announced:

> We watched and encouraged Tom Walkinshaw and his team last year when they scored four ETC victories in their first season with the XJ-S. This year they will receive our formal support.

Both statements, in fact, were less than transparently honest, for we now know that Jaguar actually gave two complete XJ-S cars to the fledgling team, and that from day one Walkinshaw was able to visit engineers to talk through his problems, referring back to what had been learned in the XJ5.3C programme. There was no way that he could approach Broadspeed, in fact, for by this time Ralph Broad had retired to Portugal, and his business was about to close down.

Walkinshaw therefore went back to his Oxfordshire base, secured major sponsorship from a French oil company, Motul, and began the preparation of a single XJ-S for the 1982 ETC series. It was all done on a shoestring at first – until mid-season there were no test cars, and no spare cars!

1982: A STEEP LEARNING CURVE

Because of the way that Group A regulations were written, the TWR XJ-S had to be developed from the ground up, differently and from a different stand point. In some ways (as in suspension and braking alternatives) there was more freedom, but the wheels and tyres had to be able to fit into the existing wheel-arch dimensions. Not only that, but the cars could only use transmissions that had been homologated.

Alternative cylinder heads and related fittings were no longer authorized, which meant that cars had to rely on their original-equipment engines being strong and suitable for power-tuning. Not only that, but race engines were obliged to use the same fuel supply system (in Jaguar's case, Lucas fuel injection) and manifolding as the road cars.

Walkinshaw, however, was not only extremely experienced in race craft, but soon persuaded Jaguar to help him with some inventive homologation. In 1982, for instance, you or I might only be able buy an XJ-S HE with automatic transmission, but Walkinshaw always used manual transmissions – at first the old-style four-speeder, but later he somehow ensured that an alternative five-speed manual gearbox appeared on the homologation form – this being a five-speed Getrag gearbox. Not only was this politically wise – for Jaguar were just about to specify a Getrag gearbox for the first of their new-generation six-cylinder XJ-S 3.6 models – but it was also pragmatic, as Getrag were already deeply involved in production car racing, their products being used extensively by BMW.

Except for its BBS-style centre-lock racing alloy wheels, and a wickedly purposeful colour scheme with the 'Motul' sponsorship emblazoned on the doors and the bonnet, and 'Akai' on the flanks, the very first TWR XJ-S race-car looked near standard. But it was not. Under that sleek skin, the 5.3-litre engine had already been tuned to give more than 400bhp, and seemed to handle at least as well as the last of the Broadspeed XJ5.3Cs. Walkinshaw told *Autosport's* Matthew Carter in March 1982:

> The Jaguar engine will rev to 8,500rpm, but we have put it on a limit of 7,200rpm and we believe we will have around 400bhp to play with. The engine will produce over 500bhp but for endurance racing we did not want the extra 100bhp.

More important, too, was the fact that it was ready – race-ready, that is – when Walkinshaw promised, unlike the Broadspeed cars, which had been previewed in March 1976 but did not actually start a race until September! This time, too, there were fewer problems in getting down to the weight limits – under Group 2 rules the XJ5.3C was allowed to aim for 1,280kg (2,816lb) but never got within 100kg of that figure, whereas the XJ-S was almost down to the 1,400kg (3,086lb) limit imposed by Group A.

When TWR unveiled their Group A racer in March 1982, it had not yet done much testing, so the 400bhp power output was decidedly provisional, and the team was still hoping to get up to a racing fuel consumption of at least 6mpg (47l/100km). Only one car would race at first, but a second car was to be ready by mid-season – assuming, of course, no accidents happened in the meantime.

It was typical of Walkinshaw, and TWR, that no vainglorious promises were made for the project, but that the car was almost immediately race-ready on its first appearance, which was the Monza 500km event. Even though there would be reliability and team problems, it would always be competitive.

Partnered by 'Chuck Nicholson' (whose real name was Charles Nickerson), Walkinshaw put the Motul car on the front row of the grid, alongside the most competitive of the BMW 528s which were to be the Jaguar's biggest competition throughout the season.

This single car led until half distance, until it went off over the trackside kerb of a chicane, the result being a split oil union under the gearbox, which caused the transmission to break and the car to retire.

A week later, and still in Italy, the XJ-S sat on pole position at the Vallelunga 500km race, set fastest lap in the race itself, but finished third behind the winner BMW of Grano/Kelleners (which actually won the first five races in the series).

In the ETC the first TWR victory did not come until June, on the Brno road circuit in Czechoslovakia, but by that time the XJ-S had already raced six times, led several races, and had already been dogged by bad luck. After Walkinshaw had won a non-championship event at the Belgian Zolder event in April, who could have forecast that victory in the Donington 500km in May would be lost by a holed radiator?

Victory in Czechoslovakia was followed by second place in Austria (when Walkinshaw drove the whole 3½-hour race alone), and just a week later there was a magnificent win over six hours of racing on the classic Nürburgring track, where the Jaguar beat the massed might of works BMWs on their home ground.

The second car duly appeared in time to start the gruelling 24-hour event on the Spa F1 circuit of public roads, in the Belgian Ardennes, but this was an event Jaguar would rather forget, for both of them crashed! Walkinshaw's car was using a Getrag gearbox for the first time, but the team's contracted Dunlop tyres were not suited to the awfully wet conditions. Even though Walkinshaw had thumbed his nose at the contract and 'found' some Pirellis to use instead, it was to no avail, and both cars ended up off the road.

Fortunately for him (and for Jaguar enthusiasts) there was then a six-week gap in the racing, before at the end of the year the TWR cars finished 1–2 at Silverstone (in the TT) and in the 3½-hour Zolder race in Belgium. To use a much-hackneyed football phrase, this had been a Championship 'of two halves': up to mid-season, the BMWs had been unbeatable, but from June onwards it was always the TWR Jaguars that looked likely to win. And usually did! The record shows that they won four ETC events, finished second three times, and third once. Walkinshaw had finished third overall in the Drivers' series, and Jaguar second to BMW in their capacity class. Not bad for starters ...

1983: WORKS JAGUARS ONCE AGAIN

Jaguar, and John Egan, were now in an ideal position to build on the successes of 1982. By standing back from the first year's racing, they could have disclaimed all responsibility if the programme had been failure; as it was, it had been such a success that they could bask in the glory.

With only a little stretching of the truth, they could (and did!) say that Jaguar had let Tom Walkinshaw do his own thing in 1982, but that for 1983 they were so enthused that they would become officially involved.

And so it was. For 1983, when the competition from BMW (with the newly homologated 635CSi Coupé) would be more intense,

By 1983 the TWR XJ-S race cars were officially factory-backed. Walkinshaw himself still found time to drive – and win – throughout the year. Along with 'Chuck Nicholson' he won this race, the Touring Car Grand Prix at Brno, in June 1983.

the factory decided to give its official backing to a two-car programme. Motul would still be a major backer, the cars would continue to be prepared at Kidlington, but there would be a stark new colour scheme – the cars being white with a broad green stripe along the flanks, and the words 'Motul' and 'Dunlop' being obvious.

Jaguar were always quite clear in their intentions – which were to prove the supremacy of their product, not just to go motor racing for the fun of it. To quote John Egan from his pre-season presentation in March 1983:

> We believe that our ETC involvement will assist our plans for sales growth in continental Europe, particularly Germany, which

is the home of our major competitors. One of these, BMW, has dominated ETC in recent years.

This time there was to be a two-car assault throughout the season. New cars were prepared, there was time for mid-week testing, and whenever possible the driver line-up was boosted by a new face – Martin Brundle, who was just on the verge of a successful F1 career. For some people, though, the Walkinshaw team was always difficult to like. In some ways, particularly in its grim, win-at-any-cost approach, the team soon became the 'black hats' of the ETC circus. Although scrutineers never complained (not, that is, in public!) the cars sometimes skirted around the edge of the regulations, and Tom Walkinshaw himself never tried very hard to put a sunny face on his relations with the press.

The XJ-S's cooling ducts for the rear axle oil-coolers were seen as illegal aerodynamic aids by some of TWR's rivals – indeed the nationalistic German press sometimes accused the team of cheating. It didn't help that one of Tom Walkinshaw's interviews, published in Germany, included the remark:

My business is to build successful racing cars and I can assure you that no one wears a totally white or totally black hat in this sport. If it's black, there are protests at every race. If it's white, you won't win. Therefore, you have to keep somewhere in between. All the successful people in this sport wear grey hats.

Auto Motor und Sport were infuriated, but chose to ignore Walkinshaw's inference – that BMW's cars might also be dubiously specified. Walkinshaw, in any case, didn't mind. Built like a bulldog, with the stubborn character to match, he was a winner who wanted to go on winning. Not only that, but in some ways he treated the TWR Jaguars as his own 'Big Boys' Toys', for he personally wanted to become European Touring Car Champion, which meant that at every race he would (and often did) swap cars around to give himself the best chance of finishing high up. No harm, in that, by the way, for 'Major Tom' (as he was known) was as pugnacious, ruthless, and effective on the track as he was in business.

FIVE WINS IN TWELVE RACES

In 1982, TWR's first Jaguar year, the season had started badly but finished well, but in 1983 fortunes were reversed. By July 1983 the team had won five of the nine races held – with Walkinshaw himself in the winning

car on four occasions – but that was the high point. Although Tom was second in the Drivers' series – one place higher than in 1982 – by his own standards he had failed, and would have to improve further in 1984.

It was a season tinged with unreliability. When motoring properly, ideally as developed and controlled, the XJ-Ss were always competitive and always battling for outright victory, but they were often foiled by breakdowns. For Walkinshaw the perfectionist, what must have annoyed him most was that some of the failures were new to the XJ-S. By no means every development problem had been eliminated (indeed, even in 1986 the cars were still likely to break down rather than finish.)

At Monza in March, for instance, the Walkinshaw/Nicholson car suffered a failed bonnet securing pin, which allowed the vast full-width panel to flap, and it needed a couple of long and rather frantic pit stops to produce any sort of solution. A Donington pit stop resulted in too little fuel being taken on from churns, the result being that the hapless Nicholson ran out of fuel. A propeller shaft shed a balance weight at Spa (when did you last see a race car have to change a prop shaft?), while a clutch failed at Zolder.

In a season marred by bad-tempered bickering between Jaguar and BMW, no other marque got a look in. In fact the *only* other marque to finish on the podium during the ETC year was Rover – and those cars were also prepared by another TWR team. Except on occasions when BMW boycotted races in a protest against Jaguar's so-called technical infringements, there was always a fleet of 635CSi Coupés to battle against two Jaguars: fortunately for TWR's drivers, the two white-and-green XJ-S team cars usually qualified ahead of the massed ranks from Bavaria and, when problems did not strike, usually only had to contend with the two or three fastest cars throughout the long races.

Ten BMWs started at Monza in March, when the Walkinshaw/Nicholson car would surely have won if the bonnet pin had not failed, while at Vallelunga Walkinshaw's car was leading when it suddenly shed a wheel. The shortfall in fuel supply at a Donington Park pit stop meant that Nicholson had to push his car over the last portion of the lap, to reach the pits.

Yet Donington Park was an important race, and an important season's turning point, for TWR. Not only did team newcomers Martin Brundle and John Fitzpatrick appear for the first time, but the XJ-S won outright. Two weeks later Walkinshaw and Nicholson won at Pergusa, in Sicily, then in mid-June the team made another successful trip behind the Iron Curtain, to Brno in Czechoslovakia. Brno, in fact, was always a 'lucky' circuit for TWR (except that 'Major Tom' didn't believe in luck, preferring to make his own) – three wins in three visits.

In four mid-summer weeks there would be three outstanding XJ-S victories – at Brno, at Zeltweg in Austria, and at the Salzburgring, also in Austria. Yet all was not sweetness and light in the ETC series, for at the prestigious Nürburgring circuit, in mid-July (when Jaguar's marketing people mounted a major promotion) both the cars retired, one with a clutch failure, the other with an electrical fault.

At this point in the season, it all fell apart for TWR, who did not win again that year. Although Walkinshaw's major rival, BMW-mounted Dieter Quester, did not win either, he scored enough points to pip the Scot for the Championship. Worse, the weather at the Silverstone TT was awful, the Jaguars' tyres could not cope, and the best TWR car could only finish eighth.

Totting up the scores, in twelve races Jaguar counted five victories and BMW six, though since Rover won the Silverstone TT, that made the score six to BL and six to the

Germans. Honours even? Not as far as Walkinshaw was concerned. He wanted to win.

1984: VICTORY AT LAST

By this time not only TWR but Jaguar also were determined to see justice done. The company was back into profit, production was booming as never before, and a high-profile privatization was on the horizon. The marketing people were in total agreement – another successful and high-profile year could only be good for Jaguar's image.

Because they carried an entirely fresh colour scheme, the 1984 works-backed TWR race cars seemed to exude an even more purposeful image than before. This time there was no doubt about the factory backing, for the cars were painted all over in British Racing Green, complete with white stripe along the flanks, and the word 'Jaguar' prominent from all angles. 'Motul' was still present, but now as a more minor sponsor.

Technically, there was change but not revolution. Having been humiliated on more than one occasion by Dunlop tyre problems, the team had taken advice from the tyre company, increasing its racing wheels to 17in diameter Speedlines with 13in 'garden roller' rim widths: this also provided the opportunity to enlarge the brake discs – to no less than 14in diameter.

By this time, too, the team had developed a water-cooling system for the four-calliper AP brakes, which entailed each car carrying a six-gallon water container on board that was replenished at pit-stop time.

Before the end of the year the seventh XJ-S race car would have started its racing career. The team needed this sort of construction, not only to make up for crashes and old age, but because no fewer than three team cars were to be entered for each

The 'works' TWR XJ-S Group A race cars adopted a new, mainly British Racing Green with a broad white stripe, colour scheme in 1984, the season in which Tom Walkinshaw himself won the European Driver's title. By then the engine's power output had risen to 450bhp, and the XJ-S cars were always competitive, winning seven of the season's 12 races. This particular car was that shared by Walkinshaw and Hans Heyer on several occasions. Note the 17in Speedline wheels.

race in the increasingly popular ETC series. As before, the principal opposition would come from the massed ranks of BMW, though a team of turbocharged Volvos ('Stockholm taxis', as they were so predictably nicknamed at the time) joined in later.

One new name to join the driving team was Hans Heyer of Germany, a previous ETC Champion himself, and intended to be Walkinshaw's high-profile partner throughout the year, while Dorset motor trader Win Percy was another.

Surprisingly, Jaguar claimed no more power than before – the pre-season 1984 press release mentioned 400bhp without quoting an rpm figure, but the maximum torque was an impressive 350lb/ft at 5,000rpm. That combative engine designer, Harry Mundy, by then retired and tending his magnificent garden in suburban Warwickshire, must have smiled thinly at this. When he had led the design team in the 1960s, he thought that a conversion from twin-cam to single-cam head, and part-spherical to recess-in-crown combustion chamber, would render the engine quite unsuitable for race-tuning.

Clearly he had been wrong – but, then, engineering design and logic did not allow for people like Tom Walkinshaw. In fact, when *Autocar* tested one of the race cars in 1985, the engine output was quoted at 450bhp at 6,750rpm, with the peak torque of 390lb/ft occurring at 4,900rpm. Peak race revs were 7,200/7,300rpm, with still a bit of margin above that if needed.

Looking back at 1984, in which Tom Walkinshaw gained the European Touring Car Championship he had coveted for so long, this was certainly a year for Jaguar and TWR to be proud of. This time Jaguar won seven of the twelve races to BMW's four – and along the way there were a couple of 1–2–3 finishes, and five second places in all. Not only that, but there was sweet revenge in winning – at last – at Monza in April, and in the Spa 24-hour race in July.

Yet for TWR this was probably the roughest season of races so far. So much was now at stake, and drivers were so competitive, not to say ruthless, that there seemed to be a great deal of car-to-car contact, and an overall atmosphere of broad-shouldered

In the European Touring Car Championship of the mid-1980s, no car was ever more impressive than the TWR XJ-S. In 1984 Tom Walkinshaw won the drivers' title in these formidable 450bhp machines. Seven such cars were eventually built – and all survived into the mid-1990s.

and rather bristly aggression. It all made for enthralling competition – and spectating – but it certainly destroyed the last old myths about gentlemanly racing.

It all started well at Monza on 1 April when the formidable new Walkinshaw-Heyer partnership beat a phalanx of BMWs: more importantly, this was done in very wet conditions, which showed that Dunlop had certainly shrugged off their earlier TWR tyre-grip problems. The team then got its tyre choice slightly wrong at Vallelunga a week later, but nevertheless hung on to finish third.

Then came the team's truly golden period – one whose script might almost have been written with publicity for the privatization period in mind! On five consecutive occasions – from Donington on 29 April to Austria's Salzburgring on 1 July – a dark-green XJ-S won the race, there were two 1–2–3 finishes, and no fewer than four second places.

What must have made this doubly galling for the opposition was that the TWR cars were quite patently race-legal, as the scrutineers were always giving them a very detailed inspection before and after the events. There was not, and never had been, any cheating here. Quite simply, the XJ-S won so often in European touring car races during the 1980s because it was the best car for the job. It might have been heavy but it was also extremely powerful. It might have been bulky but it was also extremely agile. The race cars were also crewed by the best possible drivers – and the TWR team was one of the most professional in the business.

Then it all went wrong at the 'New' Nürburgring (cynics later suggested this was inevitable, for Jaguar had chosen this race to make a major marketing push, and have many honoured guests present!), but there was sweet revenge at the demanding Spa-Francorchamps 24-hour race. Wisely, perhaps, TWR had entered only two cars but

nominated three drivers for each of them, and didn't try to make the pace in the early hours when the circuit was so slippery.

Enzo Calderari later spun one of the cars during the night, hitting a barrier and causing a lot of damage, but the Walkinshaw/Heyer/Percy XJ-S kept going. By daybreak on the second day, the weather improved considerably and the XJ-S surged back into the lead, eventually winning by three whole laps.

It was a poor year for weather, for in the Silverstone TT monsoon rain claimed two of the Jaguars (one to a crash, the other to engine failure thought to be due to ingested water), while another mid-race storm affected the Belgian Zolder race.

At the end of the year, however, the XJ-S had proved itself beyond any doubt, the abiding impression being of the dark green cars always qualifying at the front of the massed grids, and always surging away into the lead in the early laps.

RACING IN THE FAR EAST

With the ETC title won at last, and with a change to campaigning specially designed purpose-built XJR-6 racing sports cars due to follow in 1985, Walkinshaw and the team could relax for a time.

An attractive offer to send two TWR team cars to compete in the 95-mile (153km) 'Grand Prix of Macau' around the streets of that Portuguese colony not far from Hong Kong was too interesting to ignore, however, especially as there would be much financial support from the JPS cigarette brand, and competition from two of the Schnitzer BMW 635CSi race cars.

The outcome was a brisk 1–2 victory for the XJ-S machines, liveried in JPS black and gold like the Lotus F1 cars had often been. One day, perhaps, you might have to answer a 'not-many-people-know-that' quiz question and, yes, this *was* the only time TWR raced in JPS colours!

At this point the small and distinctive fleet of XJ-S race cars was retired – or, rather, put into store in case they were ever needed again. Except for maintenance, no further development was ever carried out. In the spring of 1985 one of them was taken to the Millbrook proving ground for *Autocar*'s benefit, where (with a high 3.07:1 final drive ratio) Tom Walkinshaw himself recorded an all-out lap of the two mile banked circle at 176.16mph (283.44km/h), with Michael Scarlett alongside him recording the figures.

Even with that high axle ratio and a hard-worked clutch fitted, the green race car recorded a 0–100mph sprint in 9.8 seconds, and 0–150mph in 21.5 seconds. Impressed? Of course – but think how much more remarkable these figures might have been if one of the low (3.77:1) axles had been fitted! Amazingly, the opportunity to use them in the most famous touring car race of all – the Bathurst 1000 on the Mount Panorama circuit west of Sydney – came in 1985. Even more amazingly, the three works XJ-S cars that lined up at the start were three of the self-same cars whose careers had ended so triumphantly nearly a year previously.

It was the first all-Group A race to be held at Bathurst, which meant that domestic V8-engined opposition from Holden and Ford was at a disadvantage. Back in their familiar green-with-white-stripe colour scheme, two of the three XJ-Ss sat on the front row of the grid, and throughout the long race the V12 engined machines were in control.

One car retired early on with a damaged engine (thought to be due to ingesting debris from the car's nose as it was nudged by a competing Holden), but the other pair carried on. In the end there was the best possible result for the team, for the winning XJ-S was driven by local man John Goss (who had previously driven his own XJ-S in early Bathurst races) and by Armin Hahne.

JAPAN AND NEW ZEALAND – 1986/1987

Once again the cars went back into stock at Kidlington, and once again they spent months being gently fettled for a future outing, though as the current Group A regulations were due to be revised, this would have to be before the end of 1986.

That chance did not come until a year later, when TWR were first attracted by an invitation to return to Bathurst, then dropped that idea, and opted to contest a five-hour Group A race at Fuji, in Japan, instead.

This outing, partly funded by the New Zealand-based Strathmore group, took place on 9 November 1986, and saw two of the now-venerable (and, frankly, obsolete) XJ-Ss qualifying at the head of the grid: one almost wrote 'as usual', so competitive had these cars always been over the years.

Although the Jaguars led the race from the start, neither was to finish. Was it old age, or just the character of the old cars crying out for a rest? One, certainly, blew its engine after only six laps – most unusual for an XJ-S – while the other broke its differential, which was also quite exceptional for a big Jaguar.

If the New Zealand sporting authorities had not decided to extend Group A in their own country, that would then have been the absolute end of the XJ-S's racing career. Who knows what hand Strathmore had in this decision, especially as New Zealand's ex-F1 World Champion Denny Hulme was due to drive one of the cars?

The fact was, however, that in the first weeks of 1987 two special Group A races were created in New Zealand, so that the

The TWR XJ-S race cars – a five-year record

The very first TWR-prepared Group A specification XJ-S race car started its career at Monza in March 1982. The last raced in New Zealand in January 1987. Between those dates, seven different cars raced all round the world, winning in places as far apart as Britain and Australia.

In 1985 the cars raced only once – at the famous Australian Bathurst race (which they won) – two of the same cars then resting for a full year before being sent to Japan in the autumn of 1986. The same two cars were then shipped to New Zealand, where their career ended.

Here is the complete record of that impressive career:

Event	Driver(s)	Position
1982		
Monza, Italy	Walkinshaw/Nicholson	DNF
Vallelunga, Italy	Walkinshaw/Nicholson	3rd
Zolder, Belgium	Walkinshaw	1st
Donington Park, UK	Walkinshaw/Nicholson	DNF
Mugello, Italy	Walkinshaw/Dieudonne	DNF
Brno, Czechoslovakia	Walkinshaw/Nicholson	1st
Zeltweg, Austria	Walkinshaw	2nd
Nürburgring, Germany	Walkinshaw/Nicholson	1st
Spa, Belgium	Walkinshaw/Nicholson/Percy	DNF
	Dieudonne/Allam/Lovett	DNF
Silverstone, UK	Walkinshaw/Nicholson	1st
	Allam/Lovett	2nd
Zolder, Belgium	Walkinshaw/Nicholson	1st
	Allam/Dieudonne	2nd

Tom Walkinshaw finished third in the European Touring Car Championship.

1983		
Monza	Walkinshaw/Nicholson	2nd
	Dieudonne/Calderari	DNF
Vallelunga	Nicholson/Dieudonne/Walkinshaw	3rd
	Walkinshaw/Calderari	DNF
Donington Park	Fitzpatrick/Calderari/Brundle	1st
	Walkinshaw/Nicholson	5th
Pergusa, Italy	Walkinshaw/Nicholson	1st
	Calderari/–	DNF
Mugello	Walkinshaw/Fitzpatrick	3rd
	Calderari/Nicholson	DNF
Brno	Walkinshaw/Nicholson	1st
	Calderari/Dieudonne	6th
Zeltweg	Walkinshaw/Brundle	1st
	Dieudonne/Calderari	2nd

Nürburgring	Walkinshaw/Nicholson	DNF
	Calderari/Dieudonne/	
	Walkinshaw	DNF
Salzburgring, Austria	Walkinshaw/Nicholson	1st
Spa	Walkinshaw/Dieudonne	DNF
	Percy/Calderari/Brundle	DNF
Hockenheim	Calderari	1st
	Walkinshaw	DNF
Silverstone	Walkinshaw/Dieudonne	9th
	Nicholson/Dieudonne	DNF
Zolder	Walkinshaw/Brundle/Percy	8th
	Percy/Dieudonne/	
	Calderari	DNF

Tom Walkinshaw finished second in the European Touring Car Championship.

1984

Monza	Walkinshaw/Heyer	1st
	Brundle/Calderari	13th
	Percy/Nicholson	DNF
Vallelunga	Walkinshaw/Heyer	3rd
	Calderari/Nicholson	8th
	Percy/Schlesser	DNF
Donington Park	Percy/Nicholson	1st
	Brundle/Schlesser	5th
	Walkinshaw/Heyer	9th
Pergusa	Calderari/Brundle	1st
	Walkinshaw/Heyer	2nd
	Percy/Nicholson	3rd
Brno	Walkinshaw/Heyer	1st
	Percy/Nicholson	2nd
	Calderari/Sears	3rd
Osterreichring	Walkinshaw/Heyer	1st
	Percy/Nicholson	2nd
	Sears/Calderari	DNF
Salzburgring	Percy/Nicholson	1st
	Calderari/Sears	2nd
	Walkinshaw/Heyer	DNF
Nürburgring (New)	Nicholson/Heyer/	
	Walkinshaw	5th
	Heyer/Sears	DNF
	Percy/Calderari	DNF
Spa	Walkinshaw/Heyer/Percy	1st
	Calderari/Sears/Pilette	DNF
Silverstone	Calderari/Sears	2nd
	Walkinshaw/Heyer	DNF
	Percy/Nicholson	DNF

Zolder	Walkinshaw/Heyer	3rd
	Calderari/Percy	4th
	Nicholson/Percy	DNF
Mugello	Brundle/Calderari/Sears	5th
	Walkinshaw/–	DNF
	Percy	DNF
Macau GP	Walkinshaw	1st
	Heyer	2nd

Tom Walkinshaw won the European Touring Car Championship, with Hans Heyer second overall.

1985

Bathurst 1000, Australia	Hahne/Goss	1st
	Walkinshaw/Percy	3rd
	Allam/Dickson	DNF

1986

Fuji, Japan	Walkinshaw/Percy	DNF
	Hahne/Hulme/Walkinshaw	DNF

1987

Wellington, New Zealand	Walkinshaw/Percy	DNF
	Hahne/Hulme	DNF
Pukekohe, New Zealand	Percy/Hahne	2nd

NB The name of racing driver 'Chuck Nicholson' was a pseudonym: his real name was Charles Nickerson.

XJ-Ss that had competed in Japan could be air-freighted south to race once again. In Wellington, in that city's four-hour race, both cars were competitive, well on the pace, but both retired – one with damage after encountering tyre problems and hitting a barrier, the other because of yet another axle failure.

The last appearance of all, at Pukekohe on 1 February 1987, saw just one XJ-S start a 500km Group A race. Win Percy and Armin Hahne drove the car, which finished a close second behind the winning Holden Commodore.

And that really *was* that. Amazingly, not a single car had been written off in the five-year period, though Nicholson's badly crashed TT machine had never raced again after it was repaired. Years later *Classic Cars* sampled a surviving example – actually it was XJ-S Car 004, which had been the very last car to compete, at Pukekohe, and TWR confirmed that at the time they had only sold two of the seven cars – one to Jaguar-enthusiast Campbell McLaren, the other (004) to Tony Kember, but this soon changed. By the time this book was written, Tom Walkinshaw retained only one machine – No 007, which was the 1984 European Championship winning car. Rarely seen in public, this rests warm and peacefully, in the Walkinshaw collection 'somewhere in Oxfordshire'.

10 Today's XJ-S

For everyone thinking of buying a 'classic' (for which read ten- to fifteen-year-old) XJ-S, I have one very simple piece of advice. Buy now – values will inevitably rise in the future. With the model now out of production, and with the vast majority of surviving examples in North America, demand in the world is bound to increase.

When this book was being written to coincide with the end of XJ-S production in 1996, you could pick up a perfectly usable early example – 150mph (240km) top speed, 10mpg (28l/100km) thirst, dodgy British Leyland build quality and all – for £2,500, or a lot less if it was very rusty. Now that is a ludicrous price.

Both the tail lamp clusters and the alloy wheels are vulnerable to damage in old age – and both are expensive to replace!

In the same period, even a rusty old E-Type would set you back £15,000. Pundits, though, will tell you that that hard-to-define feature, the 'market place', is always right, but I beg to differ. Am I really expected to believe that an E-Type is worth five times as much as an XJ-S? When there are plenty of both models on the market, plenty of spares available, and expertise is oozing out of every one-make club? No, I will not believe that.

Except for pointing out that the last (and by definition, the best) XJ-S cars will lose most of their initial value in the first few years – which means that *someone* will have to absorb up to £45,000 of depreciation – there is much to be said for buying a car now before opinions change, the XJ-S becomes fashionable again, and enthusiasts begin to play 'catch up'.

However as gentlemen, they say, never discuss money, perhaps I had better ignore the financial 'worth' of an XJ-S, and concentrate on what cars are available, and which are most desirable.

WHERE TO LOOK AND WHAT TO BUY

First of all, a brief look at fashions, and at XJ-S production figures. Although I personally have never understood why drop-top cars should be considered more desirable than fixed-head coupés (not in the UK, at any rate, where we do not have the predictable weather found in California, Arizona or Australia), I seem to be in a minority. Accordingly, the good news for you all is that many XJ-Ss had fold-back roofs.

Because many XJ-S cars were sold in the USA – although perhaps not as many as Jaguar's planners had hoped, way back when the car was being planned in the early 1970s – today's supply is better over there,

especially in the 'sunshine states' where bodyshell rusting is not a serious problem.

To refine the figures quoted in Chapter 7 and in the appendices, I have worked out what proportion of XJ-S cars were sold where:

Body type	Numbers built	Numbers sold in USA (& percentage of total)
Coupé	79,371	33,493 (42 per cent)
Cabriolet	5,013	1,912 (38 per cent)
Convertible	30,946	23,819 (77 per cent)
Total	115,330	59,224 (51 per cent)

This confirms that almost exactly half of the XJ-S types ever made were originally sold in the USA. However, because of the way that rust-free examples seem to survive over there, I would guess that an even higher proportion of surviving cars are still over there. Anyone considering going down the well-trodden route of reimporting a car from the USA to the UK should be reminded that the USA specifications, particularly in regard to the engine settings, may be different from those of UK-spec cars.

Coupé, Cabriolet or Convertible?

The first and most important point to make is that there was a world of difference – if not in performance and basic refinement, then in equipment, build quality, versatility, and in general market image – between a 1976 XJ-S and a 1996 XJS. The fact is that this was a car conceived and engineered at a time when British Leyland were entering their worst period, whereas in the 1980s and 1990s there were real improvements made almost every year.

Other authors have stated that it was the arrival of the HE that saved the XJ-S – true enough, you only have to study the sales figures to confirm that – but I also make the point that it was the arrival of open-air XJ-S derivatives that changed a car into a desirable range of cars. Once again, you only have to look at sales and production figures to prove that.

There are big differences in character between early and late models. The original late-1970s machines were fast and sporting, but had under-developed steering and perhaps too-soft suspension settings. Later the suspension was firmed up, performance was maintained while the weight, equipment and overall refinement of the basic design was all enhanced, and the final cars were superb GT machines, and could be had with or without firmer and more sportscar-like handling packages.

Not only that, but by the end of the car's run, an enthusiast had to choose between engine types, transmission options, body styles and a whole lot more. If you are interested in becoming an XJ-S owner today, you will need to read this book very carefully to work out just what is available.

Having said all that, unless the XJ-S is to break with every classic car tradition, it is certain that the convertible is sure to become the most sought-after version in later years. Although the coupé always had effective air-conditioning, and would therefore be suitable for use in all climates, it will never generate the same following.

Logically, though, which car is best for what purpose?

Convertibles will always appeal to those who worship open-air motoring, and who think they can trust the weather! Jaguar's own-brand examples have good torsional rigidity, which means that scuttle shake and unpredictable handling just do not figure on that car.

I will readily admit that I have not driven a Hess & Eisenhardt conversion, but received advice is that these particular cars are not as rigid as the factory model, their bodies were not built to the same levels of body quality, and they do not have the same details of body detailing. H & E examples (USA only) will always be 'desirable' because of their rarity – in round figures, there were 2,000 H & E cars, and over 30,000 Jaguar-built types – but I have no doubt that the factory convertible is a better car. Parts supply is already a problem with H & E cars, and in years to come that problem is certain to worsen.

Cabriolets are likely to attract specialist interest in future years, but during the life of the XJ-S they were firmly marginalized by the convertible, which in my opinion was a much more practical proposition.

Although the cabriolet can offer you a clear choice of open-top or coupé motoring, it is not ideal in either guise. Running as a coupé, with roof and rear panels in place, the cabin is significantly smaller than in the real coupé, and when running as a soft-top there is still something of a cramped feel all around, with steel panels, rear quarter and overhead structures all getting in the way of the sunshine. The good news is that the cabriolet has quite a stiff body shell, though apparently the late-model convertibles are stiffer still.

Coupés, as already explained, are likely to be the least popular of all types, though I really cannot understand why. That probably tells you more about me, and my desire for calm, blast-free motoring, than the prevailing fashion for surging around in an open car with the wind mussing up your hair and making a lot of noise!

Of all XJ-S types, the coupé has the largest cabin, the best possible cockpit environment, the most storage space, the highest level of refinement, the highest top

Careful detailing on the rear corner of an XJSC of the 1980s. In the mid-1990s this can all be replicated at restoration time, but supply problems are likely to increase in the years to come.

speed, and on top of this is certainly the most silent of all types.

Engines – V12 or Straight 6?

You have to strike a balance here between power output, refinement, fuel consumption and image. In bald terms, the V12 engine provides more performance and worse fuel consumption than the AJ6/AJ16 'six', while the six-cylinder engine provides good performance by any comparison *except* that of Jaguar's magnificent V12.

I have always been a huge fan of the V12, not only because it was the world's first volume-production V12 unit, but because it was so demonstrably powerful, torquey, utterly silent, and totally unfussy in everything it did. Unhappily, I also know that it

is very heavy, could be very thirsty, can be extremely costly to maintain and repair, and is absolutely not the sort of engine that a private owner can keep in peak condition all on his own.

For the private owner, I am sure the six-cylinder engined XJ-S is a more practical proposition, even though that engine is much more complex than the legendary XK engine ever was. It has electronic elements – the ECU, and the related fuel-injection controls – which are quite outside the capability of the home mechanic to maintain.

There was, of course, a world of detail difference between the V12s used in early XJ-S types, and those in late-model cars. It was not just that late-model cars were 6-litre machines, but that Jaguar engineers seemed to fight a continuous battle against

Yes, the lever really is meant to flop down again when the handbrake is set!

the legislators! No sooner were they prepared to make the engine more powerful
than they had to detune it once again to deal
with new exhaust emission or noise regulations. Then, having met those rules, they
had to redevelop the unit to deal with catalytic converters and the extra exhaust
back pressure that was inevitable.

In and around all this, there was persistent effort to make the engine more fuel efficient, not only by going over to the May-
'Fireball' combustion process, but by
working away at the fuel injection controls.
Of all the sub-derivatives of 'mainstream'
XJ-S V12s, my personal favourites were the
early-1980s HE engines, and the final 6-
litre units. However do not delude yourself
that you can ever achieve better than 15–16
(Imperial) mpg (18–19 litres/100km).

Among the six-cylinder types, I do not
think there is any argument that the 4-litre
type was a better all-round unit than the
3.6-litre, and that the AJ16 was not only
more powerful than the AJ6, but more
refined and somehow more silky as well. If
you are looking to buy a six-cylinder
engined XJ-S, therefore, you should buy the
most modern example that you can find. Of
course, if you are determined to link the six-
cylinder engine to a cabriolet, then you do
not have a choice at all.

THE COST OF OWNERSHIP

Let us make one thing very clear – it is
never going to be cheap to restore or maintain an XJ-S. Even though the car might

As ever, the interior, facia and instruments of the XJ-S are complex and carefully detailed. It's easy for a neglected example to get very tatty here, for the veneer can peel, and the leather trim and panelling can be torn or scuffed. Think of the expense when buying a car for restoration – the car might be cheap but new parts will be costly.

Because of the XJ-S shape, the flanks are very vulnerable to scraping in close parking situations. Far too many XJ-S cars hit hard times when owned by their third or fourth owners, and restoration to 'as new' condition can be a long and very costly business. This is the HE of 1981, the first to use those 'Starfish' wheels.

already have lost 70 or 80 per cent of its value in depreciation, it is still going to cost a fair fortune to restore it to health. When it was new, an XJ-S was an expensive, exclusive car – and the cost of parts and service has always been priced accordingly.

Too many hopeful buyers try to ignore this. Thinking that they are buying eternal quality, they tend to ignore the colossal expense, say, of rebuilding an XJ-S's V12 engine, of buying a replacement transmission, or even of paying for a high-mileage routine service. Do not forget, either, that badly worn suspension bushes (relatively cheap on their own) can also lead to premature tyre wear – and that fat tyres for 150mph (240km/h) cars are very costly too! This sort of care was never cheap when the cars were new, and will never be cheap in the future either.

My advice to potential XJ-S owners is to accept, right away, that they are likely to be taking on an extremely costly hobby. The fact that they may have to lay down very little capital to buy the toy does not in anyway affect the running costs, which will be extremely high.

When the time comes to rebuild the cars, most replacement parts are still available. Although major components such as the engines, transmissions and suspension items are being rendered obsolete as new Jaguar models come along, they are likely to be serviced for many years to come. Not only that, but there is a strong and long-established network of Jaguar specialists, not only in the UK and North America, but in several other countries, which has a mountain of XJ-S expertise.

Remember, too, that the V12 has been used in a whole variety of other Jaguars, and that when this book was written the AJ16-style six-cylinder engine was the mainstay of Jaguar and Daimler saloon cars. Automatic transmissions (from General Motors of the USA and ZF of Germany) and manual transmissions (from Getrag of Germany) have not only been specified on several other Jaguars, but on many other cars throughout the world, so in most cases service support for them is also guaranteed for decades to come.

Even so, I would advise anyone buying an XJ-S to purchase the service manuals and other relevant literature as well, and to make sure that the car is always regularly and properly serviced. The potential cost of letting the engines run over the proper service intervals, or of not replacing perishable items such as hoses and drive belts, can be horrific. Bodging, or patching up, will not last for long!

Detail of the final-model XJS of the 1990s, with the burr walnut wooden cappings, the 'Sport' control of the transmission, the 'cruise control' switches and the window lifts, plus the radiocassette and the air-conditioning controls ahead of the gear lever control. Caution – there's quite a lot, even in this restricted area, which may need maintenance and restoration as an XJ-S grows old.

Because the XJR-S is so rare, it is very desirable, and should hold its value better than other XJ-S types of the same period. Due to the limited production, parts supply of some of the special components may become difficult in the future.

Do not be afraid to carry out *very* regular visual and spanner checks under the bonnet, and treat any leaking liquid like a leak from your own bank account. There is so much 'pipery' in the engine bay (especially with a V12 engine installation) that there is a lot of scope for leaks. Lost water could mean engine overheating and worse. Lost fuel could mean heavy fuel consumption and a fire hazard. Do not shrug this risk off: it can, and has, happened in the past.

As ever, it is the condition of the body shell, and the supply of unique trim/furnishing components, that will provide most of the early worries. Trim parts for early (pre-HE) XJ-S types are obsolete, and

because there have been so many changes to patterns, colours and styles since then, Murphy's Law will ensure that the very piece of carpet, chrome, or woodwork that you want to replace will already be no more than a memory.

Because it would be quite possible to write an entire book about the way to restore an XJ-S, there is little scope for a survey of the myriad ways that the shell can rust away, and give problems. Let me just say that it was originally designed at a time when Jaguars were already known for their doubtful build quality, and when cost control sometimes meant making do and omitting vital rust-prevention processes.

The fact is that the body shell can, and usually does, eventually go rusty in most areas, most worryingly at high-stress points. Sills, jacking points, suspension cross-member fixings, wings, doors, and that complex scuttle/firewall area all rot away as the years progress. Later cars, particularly the restyled models of 1991–6, were much better built and protected from attack by water, salt and general filth, but none of them is likely to last for ever.

That is the bad news. The good news is that in the mid-1990s panel supply was still good, and since the shell style was only altered once, Jaguar does not have to cater for too many variables. With so many XJ-S types built in twenty years, the factory is likely to support the car for some time – and then I am sure that a specialist supplier will take over.

Finally, I have no doubt whatsoever that the XJ-S will eventually be seen as one of the classic Jaguars of all time, and that it will always be possible to maintain one, or restore one, in the manner it deserves. That unique combination of V12 power and refinement, amazingly silent 'magic carpet' ride and an unmistakable style, will live for decades to come.

Before contemplating restoration of an old and neglected XJ-S, consider the sheer volume of work, detailing and assembly needed. Incidentally, over the years there were several different steering wheels, centre consoles and seat patterns. Are you intent on originality, or just a complete car to enjoy using?

Appendix: The XJ-S Range

Production year	XJ-S 3.6 fhc	XJ-S 3.6 cabriolet	XJ-S 4.0 fhc	XJ-S 4.0 conv	XJ-S 4.0 two-plus-two	XJ-S V12 5.3 fhc	XJ-S V12 5.3 cabriolet	XJ-S V12 5.3 conv	XJ-S 6.0 fhc	XJ-S 6.0 conv	XJ-S 6.0 two-plus-two	XJR-S V12 6.0 fhc	XJR-S V12 6.0 conv	Total of XJS range by year
1975						1,245								1,245
1976						3,082					3,082			
1977						3,890								3,890
1978						3,121								3,121
1979						2,405								2,405
1980						1,057								1,057
1981						1,292								1,292
1982	18	5				3,455								3,478
1983	269	163				4,317								4,749
1984	451	199				5,852	7							6,509
1985	782	393				6,067	709							7,951
1986	650	194				6,641	1,567							9,052
1987	1,250	196				6,758	1,510	112						9,826
1988	2,066					5,045	70	3,175						10,356
1989	1,999					4,209		4,877				122		11,207
1990	1,285		41			2,939		4,633				328		9,226
1991	97		1,258	4		1,536		1,689				65		4,649
1992			1,181	1,049		352		744	12	11	1	249	34	3,633
1993			1,289	799	1,951	13		15	460	31	595	23	16	5,192
1994			985		4,633				242	28	1,030			6,918
1995			793		3,943				59	11	78			4,884
1996			120		1,485				1		2			1,608
Total by model	8,867	1,150	5,667	1,852	12,012	63,276	3,863	15,245	774	81	1,706	787	50	**115,330**

Index

Index